MYSTIC TALES
OF
LAMA TARANATHA

MYSTIC TALES
OF
LAMA TARANATHA

A RELIGIO-SOCIOLOGICAL HISTORY OF MAHAYANA BUDDHISM

BHUPENDRANATH DATTA

GYAN

Published by

GYAN

Gyan Publishing House
5, Ansari Road
Daryaganj, New Delhi-110002
Phone: 011-47034999, 9811692060
E-mail: books@gyanbooks.com

Distribution Network
gyanbooks.com
India, USA, Canada, UK, Australia

ISBN: 978-93-7225-831-8 (PB)

First Published, 1944

2nd Impression 2025

Printed at: Gyan Press, Delhi.

MYSTIC TALES OF LAMA TARANATHA
Author: BHUPENDRANATH DATTA

MYSTIC TALES
OF
LĀMĀ TĀRĀNĀTHA

A RELIGIO-SOCIOLOGICAL HISTORY

OF MAHAYANA BUDDHISM

MYSTIC TALES
OF
LĀMĀ TĀRĀNĀTHA

A RELIGIO-SOCIOLOGICAL HISTORY
OF MAHĀYĀNA BUDDHISM

by

LĀMĀ TĀRĀNĀTHA

Translated into English by

Bhupendranath Datta, A.M., Dr. Phil.

CONTENTS

SUBSTANCE OF INTRODUCTION

By Gruenwedel

The German translation of Lāmā Tārānātha's first book on India called *The Mine of Precious Stones* (Edelsteinmine) was made by Prof. Gruenwedel the reputed Orientalist and Archaeologist on Buddhist culture in Berlin. The translation came out in 1914 A.D. from Petrograd (Leningrad).

The German translator confessed his difficulty in translating the Tibetan words on matters relating to witchcraft and sorcery. So he has used the European terms from the literature of witchcraft and magic of the middle ages viz. 'Frozen' and 'Seven miles boots.'

He said that history in the modern sense could not be expected from Tārānātha. The important matter with him was the reference to the traditional endorsement of certain teaching staff. Under the spiritual protection of his teacher Buddhaguptanātha, he wrote enthusiastically the biography of the predecessor of the same with all their extravagances, as well as the madness of the old Siddhas.

Prof. Gruenwedel said that the folklore exploited for this work is not small ; it is especially noticeable in the text of the occasional news about the old ruins, temples and religion, about the destruction wrought by the followers of Islam, further the occasional informations about the relations between the Brāhmaṇicāl gods and the Buddhist Bodhisattvas and divinities. Also, there are some informative mentioning about Further-India and the manifestation of Virūpas in China. Perhaps here lies before us the iconographic agreement of the Indian Siddhas with the Sen-nin representations.

As sources of Tārānātha, he mentioned the Magadha-Panditas Indrabhadra, Indradatta and Bhataghadri instead of Bhataghati, the last two he mentioned at the end of *History of Buddhism* where Indrabhadra corresponds with his Kṣemendrabhadra.

It seems Tārānātha was much dependent on the Tibetan recipients regarding language, it is especially noticeable in connection with the proper names.

The English Translator

PREFACE BY THE ENGLISH TRANSLATOR

The book of Gruenwedel contains 212 pages of which 146 pages only cover the text. The English translation is an abstract of the text with the informative notes taken from the German translator. None of the names of the Siddhas mentioned in the text has been left out. The book contains a rigmarole of miracles and magic. Hence the important parts of the stories about the Siddhas have only been selected, else there is a repetition of the same nature. The English translator has tried to be literal, only in a few places where abstract and free translations have been made he has marked it within brackets as —('Translator)'.

The book is translated into English in an abstract form as in these days of reawakening of Indian culture, the Indian historian and the sociologist may find information in Tārānātha's books regarding Buddhist India. By perusing the Tibetan books translated into English and German it seems to the translator that all the Tibetan writers on India have used common source for their informations regarding Indian history. And in-some of these books, the authority of the Indian book Aryamanjuśrī-Mūlakalpa (translated by K. P. Jayaswal as *An Imperial History of India*) is quoted viz. the age of Pāṇini is given as contemporaneous with Mahāpadmananda of Magadha.

FOREWORD

In going through Tāranātha's books it becomes evident that he never came to India. His knowledge of Indian geography was not clear, he made mistakes about the names of persons, geographical positions of different places etc. Further, it is clear from his writings that much of what he called *Siddhis* were knowledge of alchemy, witchcraft and Blackmagic.

Again in perusing this book one will find out the process by which Mahāyāna Buddhism has gradually amalgamated itself with the Brāhmaṇism of later days which will account for the disappearance of the former from India. Indeed the Siddhis, the Sādhanās and the beliefs mentioned in his writings are still extant amongst the Hindus of present day.

The abstract translation is presented to the public so that the research student may gather some informations which may throw some further light on the history and sociology of India of that time. Again, the book containing some Indian words expressed by the Siddhas may help the philologist in his investigation regarding the languages of the period. As regards the sociological and other information culled out from this book the following are pointed out:

(1) That India had connection with the outside world at the period dealt by Tārānātha. (2) The sorcery practised in India and Europe had common forms. (3) The nature of the story of seeing in magic-mirror was common in both the places. (4) *Pa* is the Tibetan contraction of the Sanskrit word *Pād* or *Pada*. (5) *Karmaru* is the Tibetan contraction of the Indian name Kāmārupa. (6) Odivisa is Orissa, Otantapuri is Odantapuri, Udyāna or Udayāna is Udyāna (today's Cabul and Swāt valley). (7) Some of the Buddhist Siddhas carried *Jatā* (long matted hair) on their heads. (8) Tāranātha spoke of the existence of Citizens'—'Gild' of that period. (9) The use of sun-dial existed in that period. (10) Women used to sell brandy in those days. (11) The book contains instances of inter-caste marriages. (12) The wretched condition of the field-worker (peasant) in India was notorious even in those days and known to the outside world. (13) The word 'Dinar' the Indian form of the Roman coin 'Dinarius', which was used in Sanskrit literature, still persisted in the time when Tārānātha wrote this book. (14)

The book mentions a Kṣatriya-Pandita as a purohita (priest) of a king. This reminds us of the practice of the Vedic age. It lends further strength to the proof that the priesthood has not always been the sole monopoly of the Brāhmaṇas.[1] (15) The book mentions the employment of Tajik (Persian) soldiers in the service of a Rājā of Maru (Rājputanā). (16) From the list of the names of the Siddhas it will be found out that some of them were of socalled low castes.

BHUPENDRANATH DATTA

3, Gour Mohan Mukherjee Street,
Calcutta, April 1944

(1) The investigators say that in some parts of India non-Brāhmaṇas still act as priest (vide N. N. Vasu : *The Ethnology of the Kāyasthas*).

THE PUBLISHER'S NOTE

For the first time this book is now translated into and published in English from German. Originally this book was written in Tibetan by Lāmā Tārānātha and translated into German by the great scholar Prof. A. Gruenwedel. Dr. Bhupendranath Datta, the eminent research scholar in the fields of the Comparative History and Anthropology, has spared no pains to present to the reading public an English rendering from its German version. Besides being wonderfully proficient in the World History and Anthropology, his intimate knowledge in German, French and some other languages of the Continent is well-known to the learned section in India and abroad. We have no hesitation to believe that this faithful English translation from the gifted pen of Dr. Datta will be appreciated by all readers. This book openes a sealed chapter on the religio-sociological history of Buddhist India. We offer our sincere thanks to Dr. Datta for giving us kind permission to publish this important volume.

We would express our gratitude to Swāmi Sadānanda Giri for allowing us to print the pictures of Bodhisattva, Bhairava, Ganeśa and Prajñāpāramitā in this book. These were published in his valuable book: *Java-dwipa*. We are also greatly indebted to Sj. Ajita Ghose for lending us two other blocks of Vajra-Sarasvati and Atiśa Dipaṅkara. The pictures are arranged in the first page in this order: (1) Vajra-Sarasvati (A Tibetan painting) and (2) Atiśa Dipaṅkara, and in the second page (1) Boddhisattva, (2) Bhairava, (3) Ganeśa (Tāntric), and (4) Prajñāpāramitā.

15-8-44

Ramakrishna Vedanta Math
19B, Raja Rajkrishna Street,
Calcutta

MYSTIC TALES
OF
LĀMĀ TĀRĀNĀTHA

INSPIRATION I

"Here follows a narration, which is equal to a precious jewel as it is rich in wonders, and which is endowed with seven holy inspirations, while the Jātakas contains the list of former teachers

I bow to the feet of my holy teachers. After testifying my reverence to the bands of the Gurus who following one after another exercised the life-bringing path of Vajradhara to all living beings, it was my task to glorify their lives-career as far as possible in a Sūtra. For although itself a perfect one, the tongue of which had the power to work wonders, it would be impossible to execute the fame of these men in hundred ages, yet at the command of my Guru this book is written.

As I through the presence of our teacher, the holy one, who carried the name of Buddhaguptanātha, and in remembering the Bauddhas of three ages, was entrusted with the task to unite properly all words from prose and verse in the sea of theme-building; while

I tried to keep myself everywhere within the jurisdiction of his power, where it was only possible on the power of his holy words, and there also preceded the presence of my great Siddha Guru himself, who through his holiness is a root-Guru, thus the people will be properly informed of the power, also of incorporeal power of commission of even of this man who himself has the fame to be graced with the seven inspirations of beatitudes. (P. 9).

What concerns the first inspiration was the Mahāmudrā-Revelation. Its adept was Mahācārya Brāhmaṇa-Rāhulabhadra born in the country of Odivisa. By caste he was a Bhāhmana and from childhood was confided with the Vedas and with Vedāṅgas. Going to Madhyadeśa, he professed the doctrine of Buddha and gradually became a great Tripitaka-knowing Bhikṣu. The teacher of this ācārya was Sthavirakāla, whose teacher was named the honoured Aśvaghoṣa. Though the Gurus say that the teacher of the last had been Upagupta, yet it is difficult to make a judgment over the correctness of the ancient teacher-generations. But it is extolled in the context of Tibetan lists that he was ṭhe corporal student of the son (of Gautama) of Rāhulabhadra. So it is sufficient to note here without further examination. Later, he became an abbot in Nalanda. Lastly he went to the southḥ. Thus, in the country of Mahratta he saw the Yoginī of the sphere of his work in the form of the daughter of an arrow-smith, who could extinguish the essence of his ego-existence. He knew Dharma thoroughly, gave at once the Mudrā to the daughter of the arrow-smith and prosecuted the work of arrow-making while wandering in many countries. When his wisdom began to grow more, he received the name of Śaroha, i.e., who is met with the arrow. Thus, came innumerable men with the king at the head, to see him, and they derided him. There in the posture of a Brāhmaṇa, the ācārya sang *'ah hurra,* indeed I am a Brāhmaṇa, I live with the daughter of an arrow-smith—caste or no caste, there I do not see any difference; I have taken the sworn vow of a Bhikṣu, I go a-begging together with a woman—sin or no sin, I do not see any distinction.' 'Here is an impurity', thus doubted men amogst themselves, but could not recognize that the man is poisonous as a serpent. But after he had sung the Dohā-Vajra songs the five times hundred thousand men with the king acknowledged excellently the aim of his action. As he now acquired a

Vidyādhara-body, magically he went to heaven and finally became invisible." (pp. 10-12).

Here, the author states that this Brāhmaṇa Rāhula and Sthavira Rāhula are two different persons.—(Translator).

"His pupil was the ācārya Nāgārjuna. He was born in the south in Vidharbha, by caste he was a Brāhmaṇa. Finally he came to Nalanda. As his teacher Rāhulabhadra advised him to mutter incessantly the Dhāraṇis of the Amitayus so it was possible for him to live in peace. He became a monk there. There was nothing for him to learn, as neither Mahāyāna nor Hinayāna-pitakas remained strange to him. Therefore, he exercised the Mahāmāyūrī, the Kurukulli, the nine Yakśiṇīs and the Mahākālas; he acquired all Siddhis : the globule Siddhi, the eye-ointment, the sword-Siddhi, further all power to destroy and again to revive to life, and got complete power over all superhuman Yakṣas and Nāgas and especially received a Vajra-body which was created for him by the elixir of life. He became a giant on magic power and supernatural knowledge. In various places he performed Siddhis of the sword and quicksilver-Siddhis. For the Saṅgha he created food materials as well, when the abbot Rāhulabhadra was busying himself with the exorcism of Āryatārā, Nāgārjuna came to the abbey at that time. During this period there was a famine in Magadha for twelve years. Ācārya performed a gold-tincture (Siddhi), and as far as this gold-tincture reached, the cornfields changed and there was no famine, hence the Saṅgha was not without bread.

Then he worked on many heretical hand-books viz. those which belonged to Veda-class; and fought with all enemies of Mahāyāna viz. Saṃkara, with the Bhikṣus etc. refuted them, and as well as many dialectical polemical literature written by the Saindhava Śrāvakas. He collected all the copies and buried them under the ground. Later, once he fought with five hundred Tirthikas in the city of Jātasaṃjaya, lying in the south, he defeated them and won them over to the religion. Thus he made the Mahāyāna as brilliant as the sun. Then he wished to change the Ghantaśaila and many mountains lying on the north viz. Dhinkota etc. into gold. Āryatārā dissuaded him from it as it would bring quarrel over it in future. But it is said that many gold-mines are present there, and at least the stones show the colour of gold. Later, while journeying northward he seeing many boys playing, prophesied that a boy would be a king. Twelve years later, coming back to Jambudvipa from Uttarakuru he saw one of the boys as a king named Udayāna who made reverences to him. As a consequence the king received the elixir of age and the Yakṣas as his servants. He built five hundred temple-cloisters as the resting-place of the preachers. Later, he (ācārya) dwelt on the Śriparvata for two hundred years long, surrounded by the Yakṣīs and remained there practising the Tantras till his subsequent beheading by the grandson of the king Udayāna called Susukti or the mighty prince. As it is related, it took place, in his seventy years of age, when the 71st year was not complete as it was only half-year. The mother of the prince asked his son to beg of the head of the ācārya as his father and ācārya possessed magic by which his age would be as long as the ācārya, and as the ācārya had a Vajra-body he would not die. The mother wanted it for the good of the son. The prince went to Śrīparvata and begged of the ācārya for it. The head was cut off by a Kuśa-stalk. A word was heard : 'I go from here towards Sukhavati, but will come back again and will rejoin the body.' Thereupon there were earthquake and famine for twelve years. As the prince was afraid of the rejoining of the body he threw the head many miles distant from the place of beheading. A Yakṣī took up the head, and the Yakṣī Kṣitipati built a temple over the head and body. My Lāmā has seen and narrated the following : This temple whose walls are formless and seem to be like rocks is a wonderwork. The outside of it is steep and there is no way to it. (pp. 14-19).

His disciple was Mahāsiddha Śavarī. When Nāgārjuna was staying in Bengal, a dancing-master brought there children (brother and sisters) from the east. He called them and showed the figure of Bodhisattva Mahāratnamati. As the dancing-master wanted to see also, he was shown a mirror in which he saw himself roasting in hell-fire. He wanted to be saved and was asked to meditate on Sambara. After his meditation, he recognized the original cause of his soul and recognized the face the Bodhisattva Mahāratnamuni. Then Nāgārjuna told him that as he now got power he should go to the south (Śrīparvata), live the life of a hunter and create the good of the creatures. The both sisters Logi and Guṇi got their Mudrā names as Dākinī Padmāvatī and Jñānavatī. He lived with them outwardly a sinner. He got the grace of Vidyādhara and became famous as Śavarī.

This ācārya is also called the younger Śaroha. The disciple of this ācārya was Lui-pā (Luipāda) whose disciple was Dombi, whose was Tilly, his Naro, his younger Dombi, his Kuśalibhadra (pp. 19-20). There were series of schools, Luipa, Dārikā and Antara built also another series which began with Tilo.

Luipa was a writer of the king of Udayāna in the west named Samanta Śubha. Once he met Mahāsiddha Śavarī who together with him sang a song, and received Abhiṣeka and Tantras from the latter. Once he went to a cremation place (lit. field of corpses), sat himself in the rows of the Dākinīs and made himself master of the inn (lit. a publican) and therefrom he distributed the flesh of seven corpses. As he had now received Vajravārāhī in exorcism-Maṇḍala of Abhiṣeka, he said : 'Kicking with outstretched foot I destroy the slavery of Saṃshāra, Vajrasattva is a greater king, more and more again one should set himself to business.' Later, he perceived that it would be necessary to meditate without disturbance. On that account, he went to the east, to Bengal, and when he saw on the bank of the Ganges, a hill made of heaps of fish-entrails, he meditated there for twelve years, ate the fish-entrails and acquired the Mahāmudrāsiddhi.

He also converted miraculously the king and minister of Orissā. Thereupon, the king got the name of Dārikā or Dāri, the servant of Hetaera, the minister, the name of Denki (rice-husking mill). He worked on the Denki of a brandy-selling woman. (pp. 19-23).

Another disciple of Śavarī was Maitrī or Maitrīgupta. He was a Tirthika-Paṇḍita and a Brāhmaṇa. Later he met Nāro and himself joined with the Bauddhas, received Abhiṣeka and Upadeśa and became a monk of Nalanda. Getting instructions from many great and learned Gurus like Ratnākaraśānti, he became a great Paṇḍita and dwelt in the monastery of Vikramaśīlā. Though he carried on the profession of a Paṇḍita and practised no exorcism, he beheld Vajrayoginī personally.

Once as he did not properly recognize his own nature he got a prophesy. Consequently he went to Śīparvata to see Śavarī. In his journey towards the south he met the prince Sagara. Both went towards Śrīparvata and asked everybody where was the old Siddha Śavarī. They travelled for a halfyear in this way. But as the head hair (*Jatā*) of Śavarī was lousy and possessed by nits, both the Śaktis were busying in removing these things. Maitrī for a moment was staggered, but the prince fell down at his feet. As the words resounded : '*Aya Jara Valahu*', Maitrī became at once free, received a rain-bow body and faith arose in his heart. But as again he saw that both the women were killing swines, roes and peacocks, he again became a little unbeliever ; but with the snapping of the fingers everything disappeared. Now he was given Abhiṣeka, all the Upadeśas and commenting advices being bestowed, the wisdom of knowing the region of his work dawned to him. He became the master of a number of Suras and Dākinīs, won the eight Siddhis, the sword-Siddhi etc. But as Śavarī again demonstrated to him some jugglery, he cried out ; 'why must you make these jugglery, rather explain to me the basis of the region of my work' and went at once back to Madhyadeśa.

People say that he came to Tibet. It is clear that the Tibetans are not oriented over the mainpoints of his life."

Here follows discussion over the Tibetan tradition—(Translator).

"In his seventieth year of age he left his body after receiving the Mahāmudrā in the meantime. In the time when ācārya Nāro had left the body, he had appeared as the leader of the healer of the souls. People owe him still greater advancement than equalling him with the greatest. As in Āryadeśa at that time there was no aim which the people could follow, he worked in the northern countries of Nepal and Tibet with greater success. He had four great disciples: Sahajavajra or Natekana, Śunyatāsamādhi or Devakara Candra, Rāmapāla, and Vajrapāṇi known also as 'Indian Pani'. The first two and the fourth rceived corporeal Vidyādharīs. Rāmapāla of the school of Nandapāla who made commentaries on the books on Abhiṣekas was born in Karnāta as a Brāhmaṇa. He knew the Vedas. Maitrī taught him for twelve years. He had in his possession a goddess or a Yoginī who possessed the power of a Śakti. To him prayed ācārya Kuśalibhadra the younger and Asitaghna for Mahāmudrā instructions.

Here closes from the history which is equal to a mine of precious stone the first chapter over the occasion of Mahāmudrā-Tradition." (pp. 23-28).

INSPIRATION II

"Now comes the second inspiration which comes from the goddess Chaṇḍikā, but as there was no Upadeśakas of Chaṇḍikā, the inspiration worked magically.

One of the Siddhas was Virūpa. There is no proof to show that he had a Guru by a separate person. He applied himself one day personally to Vajrayoginī when this ācārya Panditabhiṣu was in Nalanda. He allowed himself the pleasure of drinking brandy, cohabited with a woman and was driven out of the monastry by the Saṅgha. Then he asked a ferryman on the shore of the Ganges to take him to the other side; but it happened so that, he having no fare for the ferry, showed his pointing finger to the Gaṅgā and the Gaṅgā stood up straight. Thus he came to the other side. Then in Odica, he demanded brandy from a wine-selling woman and as this one said he must pay the bill, he began to chase the shadows of a sun-dial from the fields but which did not go away from there, so he pointed his finger towards the sun and held it as with a nail and drunk brandy. As he did not want to set it free, the clocks and the guards made mistake. The king who knowing that the Yogī wanted to show his power, gave the price for the brandy and prayed to him to let the sun loose. Three days after he went away in the morning.

After that, as the sacrifice festival of a king of Triliṅga was being made, he consumed the first offerings of the Tirthikas, but he made no reverence thereby. As the king and his people protested to him, he bowed but all the statues of the gods of the Tirthikas broke into pieces. There the prince of the gods was a Liṅga form, a limb consisting of four faces called Visvanāṭha, establised by the people of the citizen-gild, and this one was also broken into four pieces. After that, he went to Dākinipātha in the house of the Tirthika-Gaṇas. Though lots of persons were there, the *Triśūla* was held by him as the main-article for slaughter and the witches already built Gaṇas to the flesh (offering?) of Śiva, there the ācārya clapped his hands and the *Triśūla* broke. As now the self-erected stone image of the Chaṇḍikā slightly shaking began to move, there with a blow on the head, he went with head on her brest to the womb. People say that he is still there, kneeling in straight position, but his pair of ears are only to be seen. He ordered her, not to bring ạny living being to destruction.

Now it is onesided opinion of the Tibetans, that this Dākinīpātha lay in the south, but it seems that, it was in eastern India. Further it is also said that the converter of the goddess had been Gorakṣa.

"As after that he went to Sorasta, there was a self-erected (Sayambhu?) stone image of Maheśvara called Somanātha, very strong in miracles. As he thereby did not wish to break it, he with his pointing finger proved that the figure of Avalokiteśvara had appeared on the statue. Some say that it has been the figure of Mārīchī" Then followed further miracles.—(Translator).

"Sometime later as he lived in the time of king Rāmapāla and carried the name of Siro, he rendered all possible help to the living creatures in Madhyadeśa. As he washed his own feet, Vānvādala, the elephant of king Rāmapāla drank the water, then went to the battle and was victorious over a hundred Mleccha-princes."

Later, once in the country of Gauṛ stood a Yogī over the pillows of a Tajik prince, when he awoke. This Yogī could not be destroyed in water, fire, by weapons and by poison. Then the king recognized that he had acquired the Siddhi and asked him: 'Who art thou?" He answered :' I am Virūpa'.

Then he gave instructions to some who acquired lower Siddhis. In Bengal he stayed for four months enjoying all Siddhis; but where he went afterwards no body knows. There is an especial instance when he appeared magically in China. People say that Virūpa appeared thrice in the human world. This ācārya was named by the people as Srī·dharmapāla, but he was not identical with Sthavira Dharmapāla who was an abbot of Nalanda. (pp. 28-31).

His disciple was the man who appeared in Odiyāna as Kālavirūpa. He was scarcely born in the Brāhmaṇa caste, when the Brāhmaṇa astrologers told his parents that he would commit four mortal sins. Later, he committed four sins : murder of a Brāhmaṇa, killing a cow, sleeping with mother, drink which degrades a Brāhmaṇa. Then he wandered in all Brāhmaṇa and Buddhist temples and cloisters, but could not be absolved of sin. Then he met Jalandharī, and getting precept from Vajravārāhī was absolved of his sin. (pp. 31-33).

With Virūpa the younger was Vyādhali. He was originally of the bird catching family (Vyādhāli). He received Mudrāsiddhi in twelve years. (pp. 33-34).

He taught Kuśalibhadra, he was Chandrikā-

Tāntrika, Further Virūpa gave instructions to Dombi-Herukā. It is known in Tibet that he is identical with the ācārya of this name. But, it seems he was a king in the eastern laying country of Tripura (p. 34). The ācārya went and gave Abhiṣeka and Upadeśa to the king who meditated on his *Tattva* and got the second grade of knowledge. He recognized that he could make exorcism and as a proof worked on a Mudrikā who was of the Hetaera class. She become his Padminī. This became known to the public who said the king's family was disgraced. He was driven out of his kingdom by the minister and subjects. As he practised Vidyā-asceticism, wandered in woods and fields and therefore got the name of Dombi. Thus, Dombi is one who goes with a Hetaera. Later, there was famine in the kingom, and the virtuous king with her Śakti riding as a tigress standing on a She-Yak and himself sewed with poisonous snakes came there. The people recognized that he had become a Siddha. They became his disciples. They became Tāntrikas and acquired Siddhis (pp. 34-35).

Further, in a country called Rādha commonly called Rāḍa, there lived a king who did lots of injury to the religion of Buddha, but was very much afraid of tigers and serpents. The ācārya worked wonders and told him: 'If you do not yourself accept the religion of Buddha, then I will bring to you these poisonous snakes.' And all accepted the religion of Buddha. Thus he made an end of the continuation of the Tirthika-religion in the country of Rāṛa. Lastly, he went to sleep in his corporal form in heaven. (pp. 36-37).

His disciples were the Yoginīs of the Dombi-system. Ācārya Ālālavajra, Hemalavajra and Ratavajra were from Madhyadeśa. There were also others: Kṛṣnacāri, ācārya Garvari, Jayaśri, and Durjayacandra. (pp. 37-38).

Rāhubhadra and others touched the feet of this ācārya and acquired subtleties of Siddhi. Thus Mahāsiddhā Dombi taught a Hetaera, and this one to Ratavajra, and he to Kṛṣṇacāri, and this is a Tantra school. (pp. 38).

Rāhulavajra was a Kṣatrīya and Vikramabhikṣu Paṇḍita. He meditated on the Guhya-(esoteric) Tantras. (p. 39).

Here closes from the history which is equal to a mine of precious stone, the second chapter: the occasion of Inspiration series of Caṇḍikā." (p. 40).

INSPIRATION III

'Here follows the third Inspiration, the Karma-Mudrā. The great king Indrabhūtī was master in Guhya-Tantra.[1] He was the king of Udayāna who saw the materialized face of Buddha. He saw the Rṣis, who formed the surroundings of the master, going and coming but forming no halting places. In answer from his minister he heard that they were the Śrāvakas of the great Rṣi Buddha the Tathāgata. The king wishing to realize Buddha, gave up the enjoyment of his five senses with his wives. Miraculously before him appeared an endless Maṇḍala and the king received the Abhiṣeka. Tathāgata gave him all the Tantras. He taught all population of Udayāna and wrote the Tantras in book forms. He left the company of his wife and his own over-sensuous body and travelled from one Buddhakṣetra to another. He gave Siddhi to all men, and from animals to worms and disappeared in the Rainbow-body. (pp. 40-42).

There was a dancing-girl from Srīmat Sukha, who later became a Dākinī, saw her (mate-

1. Mahāpaṇdita Rāhula Sāṅkṛtyāna who is a great scholar of Buddhism tells the translator that there had been only one king Indrabhūti who was of Orissa (Odivisa). In that case Tārānātha must have made a mistake in calling him the king of Udayāna.

rialized) face again. She was called the Sahajasiddhi dancing-girl. (This Sahajasiddhi dancing-girl is identical with Sukhilalitā in Tārānātha's *History of Buddhism* pp. 210, 17). According to the commentary of Sahajasiddhi, she was the daughter of a king of a part of Udayāna. When she grew up, once she went with a group of five hundred girls to a garden. There appeared Bodhisattva Vajrapāṇi in a magic form of a Ṛṣi. As he was seen by the girls, they raised a cry and ran away, taking him to be a demon on account of his Ṛṣi's hair-dress (matted hair). But the dancing-girl said: 'Don't you fear' and she having a look at him went into Samādhi. Then she and her five hundred maidens bowed to his feet and he blessed them by putting his hand on their vertex. Then he preached to them with the words: 'May you all be Yoginīs.' They, according to their *Tattvas*, attained the ten Sarvadarśana-dharmas. (pp. 42-43).

After she preached to Mahāpadmavajra, this one to Anangavajra, and to the swine-keeping woman, this one to the Padmavajra Saroruha the junior, this one to Indrabhūti the junior, this one to Kṛṣṇcāri, this one to Kalyāṇanātha, this one to Amitavajra, this one to Kuśalibhadra. (p. 43).

Mahapadmavajra was born in a Brāhmaṇa caste in the western country of Maru. After knowing the *Tripitakas* and all the teaching books he went to Udayāna, and saw the (materialized) personal face of Vajrasattva. In order to get Abhiṣeka he went to the divine dancing-girl. There he wrote many Tantras for the mystery of Guhya collections and informations on four Mudrās. He also wrote a manual called *Guhyasiddhi*. (pp. 43-44).

Now follows Anaṅgavajra. He belonged to a caste of a low occupational order. He meditated for twelve years on the Kotamba mountain according to the advice of his teacher Padmavajra. The advice he got from his Guru was : 'Put yourself in touch with the swine-keeping woman by keeping swine and then step by step you will be a Vajrasattva.' He began to keep swine in a city of north Udayāna,, healed many persons and became famous as the holy swine-keeper. (p. 44).

His disciple was the ācārya Saroruha belonging to the Kṣtriya caste. As he was a great Paṇḍita and knew the sciences and many Guhya-Tantras, he became the sacrificing priest (Purohita) of the king. Once seeing him in the company of a common woman of the temple, the king ordered them to be burned. But out of the ashes, he reappeared as

Herukā with Śakti in a halo of brilliant rays. Thus, the people were surprised and became converts to Vajrayāna (cult). The king also with five hundred people acquired the Siddhi. Later the ācārya went in the neighbourhood of Maru. Seeing the miraculous power of the ācārya, the king professing the Tirthika religion accepted the religion of Buddha. A temple of Herukā was built, and it was solemnly predicted of him that if he gave up his vows and wanted to see the veiled figure, he would die by spitting blood. But when later, he wanted to destory it with his Tajik (Iranian) soldiers, twelve Tajik cavalrymen fell down at the same time and he became insane. But the ācārya brought immense blessing to all creatures and acquired the Siddhi of Hevajra. (pp. 45-49).

His disciple was king Indrabhūti the junior. But as he himself ordered to narrate the burning of the ācārya, his life-history was not completely described. It was written as an occasional comment on the margin of the history of Kambala."

Here closes from the history which is equal to a mine of precious stone, the third chapter on the occasion of information of hundred Karma-series." (p. 49).

INSPIRATION IV

"As regards the Inspiration of bright Rays, it was ācārya Vajraghanta who in Udayāna worshipped personally Vajrayogini and her suit. And concerning the old series of teachers, it was Mahācārya Aśvapāda who reached the Mahāmudrāsiddhi.

He meditated and attained deep Samādhi on the bright Ray, built a hut near a door of a city in Udayāna and worked jugglery with the king. He disappeared in celestial region by magic. (pp. 49-50).

Now prayed the king and his people to his disciple Viṇapāda for Upadeśas. This ācārya originally was of royal descent. He acquired immense Siddhi. (p. 50).

His disciple was the brandy-selling woman Vilāsyavajrā. As the king was a believer in Tirthika-doctrine, she advised the ācārya Dombi-Herukā to convert the king by threatening him with snakes. The serpent surrounded the palace of the king, and said to the king: "As the Tirthika ācārya cannot protect thee, thou seekest the help of Dombi-Herukā." The ācārya drove away the poisonous snakes under the earth. The king and his surrounding people began to believe on the Buddhas. As Dombi and Viṇapāda both saw that the brandy-selling woman was a worthy subject to be a disciple, they gave her Abhiṣeka and Upadeśas. She acquired powers and honour of a Yoginī. The Queen Lakṣmikarā gave her Mahāsukha-Upadeśas. As she served the living beings in innumerable ways, she became famous under the name of Yoginī Cintā. (pp. 50-51).

Vajraghanta also got learning from her. This ācārya was of royal blood from a country name Odivisa and became a monk in Nalanda. He received the name of Śrīmatigarbha. Later he became a great scholar, destroyed the opposition of the Tirthikas and became famous as 'Deva who triumphs over the enemies.' Once he had a high rank as an abbot of Nalanda, there he met Siddhi Dārik.

After acquiring Siddhi he went to Udayāna where he met the Yoginī Vilāsyavajrā who had taken the form of a swine-keeper. She showed him the incomprehensible way of Mahāmudrāsiddhi. He inculcated all *Tattvas* and meditated in a thick forest near Odivisa. For a time, he took as his Mudrika, a brandy-selling woman who possessed all the signs of a Padmini. After twelve years of meditation, the ācārya received the honour of an adept of the highest Mahāmudrāsiddhi.

In order to keep the unbelievers at a distance and to determine the sphere of virtuous merit for the future creatures he put up a stone image of Avalokiteśvara and to circulate further the Guhya-Tantras, he exorcised once a son and a daughter. Hearing this, the king ordered the brandy-selling woman to bring the ācārya. As the ācārya entered through the east door of the city, magically the ācārya with Śakti appeared as Herukā with Śakti. The boy and the girl changed themselves into Vajra and Ghanta, he took hold of them and flew to heaven. This ācārya had spread Vajrayāna in all institutions of every country and had innumerable disciples who acquired Siddhi. (pp. 51-53).

He gave lesson to Kambala. This ācārya was a son of a king. His mother-country was in Udayāna region ; some say he had been from Odivisa. When he grew up, he became a monk in a temple-monastery and became learned in *Tripitakas*. Later, once he went towards east, where he met ācārya Vajraghanta. There he received the Abhiṣeka in Cakrasambhāra and the Maṇdala of his accompanying gods. Then he reached the highest Prajñā. As he went in the west in the country of the Dakinīs, the Tirthika-Dākinīs gave a flower-garland in his hand.

As he took it, the Bauddha-Dakinīs said : 'O son, it was not good that thou hast taken the garland, they are Tirthika-Dākinīs ; as thou hast taken the flower-garland, thou must belong to them.' Thereupon he said : 'Then you must give attention to it'. Then a settlement was made between the Tirthika and Bauddha-Yoginis that from whose flowers anybody would be hit first, to them would belong the concerning person."

Then followed lots of magic wonders.—(Translator).

"The attention of the Dakinis could not damage him. After that, the time came for the ācārya to practise on the field of dead bodies ; he went in the Śmaśāna of five hundred Montra-holding (Dākinī-) princesses in the country of Uadyāna. There was a certain Mantravatī experienced in the Mantras of Sahajasiddhi and magic-powers, she was a Hexe (witch). She wanted to destroy the ācārya and his followers and attempted to seize him ; but could find nothing but a piece of woollen-cloth (Kambala) on the spot where the ācārya sat. The witch saw that this was a magic work of the ācārya that he had transformed his own body into a woollen-cloth ! 'That must be torn off and everybody must eat a piece of it.' With these words she tore off the cloth and everybody (of her following) ate off a piece. Thereupon the ācārya made himself again visible and cursed them all, and five hundred witches with Mantravatī became five hundred sheep-headed Mātṛkās."

The transformed witches complained to the king, but the ācārya made them disgorge the woollen-cloth. (Translator).

"As they ate up his body, he became known under the honourable name of Kambala. Then he gave Abhiśeka to king Indrabhūti, who acquired Siddhi. Here closes from the history which is equal to a mine of precious stone, the fourth chapter on the narration of the working of brilliant Rays. " (pp. 53-58).

"Ācārya Indrabhūti and ācārya Kambala both prayed with Siddha Jalandhari for the beatitude of the brilliant Rays. As regards his country, he was born in a low-class in the city called Thatha, in Sindhu, in the country of the west. By the power of the virtues, he was rich in earthly pleasures. Later, he became a Bhikṣu of a temple-monastery .Once as he was in contemplation over the Upadeśas which he had received from ācārya Kambala from his prayer, came a voice from the heaven: 'Go thou to Udayāna and meditate there; there willest thou acquire the eagerly desired Siddhi.' Thereupon he went to Udayāna, got lessons from the king Indrabhūti, the godly-lady Lakṣmīkarā and from the ācārya Kacapāda instructions in all Tantras; then for the period of meditation extending to ten days, he went to the Smaśāna, received open entrance to the Maṇḍala of Srī-Herukā and Abhiśeka from four Dakinīs, and arrived at once at the grade of Mahāmudrāsiddhi. Thereafter, he engaged himself in every way for the salvation of living creatures whilst he was living in this country for a long time.

After this, the ācārya lived in the country of Jalandhara, at the place where fire comes out between water and stones (Jvālāmukhī in Kāṅgrā valley). As he lived here for a long time he received also the name of the country and was called as Siddha Jalandhari.

Once he was in the neighbourhood of Nepal, near a place wherefrom a self-sprung Stūpa a very miraculous Liṅga of Iśvara had arisen ; he built a hut and prayed there. This Iśvara was possessed with supernatural eyes, and worked magically for the exhibition of his power by many small strokes and through acts of brutal cruelty, also he Kuśalanātha, king Līlācandra further Amitavajra, prince Lavaji and others became indescribable lordly Yogīsvaras and as they met later the Brāhmaṇa Srīdhara and his followers, they acquired the Siddhi. Ācārya Bhadra gave his teachings to Antara, he to the man who enjoyed the fame of having appeared as the destroyer of the religion of the Baudhas. To make him tractable, the ācārya went there. At that time, three kings had assembled there for the worship of this Liṅga. The ācārya went in the middle of hundred thousand men, and as he showed his index-finger to the Liṅga, its head fell down to the foot, and as he looked at it, the body broke up in many pieces. Then, the whole world recognized that he had acquired Siddhi; and they trampled the idol on foot.

Then, he went once to the country of Camparna. There was a king who wanted to destroy the monasteries. There appeared a Vīṇā-player at the gate of the palace who wished to see the king. He was let in and he commenced to play on Vīṇā and sang. As the king and his surrounding were amused at it, the Vīṇā-player transformed himself into a Yogī. As the king noticed that he would be a Bauddha who appeared as such (as he wanted) to cheat with his magic, the ācārya spoke out the Bauddha-Tantras. But the Tirthikas scolded the king, who ordered his men to cut off his head. But they could not do damage to the ācārya inspite of their all sorts of weapons. Then, as the ācārya clapped both of his hands, the palace broke into pieces, and he with his exorcising look made the people of the king benumbed and stiff. The king fell at his feet and asked him praying: 'What shall I do?' The ācārya answered: 'In order to be free from your former sins, you must do something more, so that where there was one monastery, two must be established and must allow the local monks' community to be doubled. And as long as you live, make an endowment to the Saṅghas which would be sure for seven generations and make a copper plate grant for this purpose. The king acted accordingly.

Again, in the country of Mālava was a king called Bharāhari, nowadays in people's language called Bharthāri. He possessed eighteen thousand horses and ruled over wide territories; he also had a thousand wives. The ācārya knew that the time had come to convert the king, so he put him up in a place not far from the city."

Then following a miracle. (Translator).

"The king asked the ācārya to make him his disciple. He answered: 'You leave your kingdom, make Avadhūti, then I can give instruction to you.' The king gave up everything, followed the ācārya and received Upadeśas, and shortly became a Yogeśvara. Later he with five hundred people went to heaven.

As regards the former emanations the ācārya had procured a boyish spirit, therefore, he was also called Bālapāda. As he wished once to convert the countries in the east, he took the figure of a Hāḍi—of a man who swept the streets in the city of Catigrāma in Bengal. In this country the young king Gopīcandra sat (on the throne) not very long ago. As he was very handsome, he had given himself much to the women. One morning his mother saw the ācārya in the king's fruit-garden. He was sitting at the foot of the trees and uttered the words: '*Nārikela Bhikṣavo*' and the fruits of the tree came by themselves to him. After having drunk the cocoanut water, he spoke: '*Nārikela Uparajāhi*' and the fruits went up as before.

As the mother of the king saw him doing this, she recognized that he had acquired the Siddhi. Then she considered that, this would be the time to convert the king. Once in the presence of her son, tears came into her eyes. The king said: 'Oh mother! is there anything that can be done to thee?' She answered: 'When thou hast acquired ten times the umbrella (rājaccatra), the power and clever understanding of your father, yet thou hast not got the law for escaping from death, that makes you clear that thou art self perishable'. Then the king answered. 'Is there no remedy for death?' Thereupon the mother said: 'Our street-sweeper possesses it.' Then went the king to the street-sweeper : 'Thou must give me the instruction so that no one must die.' Then what he answered was: 'When thou dost not give up thine throne, thou can never reach it.' Thereupon the king answered: 'As I have first prayed for instruction, later I will give up the kingdom.' Then both of them went to a wood. There the ācārya gave the king an empty earthen pitcher and said: 'Put thine hand into it.' and as he put his hand into it, the ācārya said ; 'Now tell me quickly what is there?' As the king answered that nothing was there, the answer he got was that the road to immortality was just like that. As the king asked three times and everytime the ācārya gave him the same information, the king was put out of temper and took him to be a cheat. The king dug a groove in the earth and filled it with thorn-bushes, elephant and horse dung and threw the ācārya there and covered him up. So, the ācārya showed a double function of his body: in Jalandhara he was wandering to work for the salvation of beings, and at the same time taught in Bengal. Later, thereupon came the ācārya Kṛṣṇacāri to Kadalīksetra which in people's mouth is called Kacali; as amongst the disciples of the ācārya Kṛṣṇacāri there were many who were Yogīs, they gave opportunity to all with the words: 'Awake, awake, it is the time to become the Siddha-disciples of Kṣṛṇcāri'. Many acquired Siddhi there, but the Siddha Gorakṣa had already achieved his Siddhi. As the ācārya came there, he begun a conversation with Gorakṣa. Occasionally in answer to Gorakṣa he said that his Guru was Jalandhari. But now twelve years had passed since Jalandhari had been put into a grave underground, he went himself there, surrounded by four times hundred thousand Mimāṅsakas towards the east. Full of rancour he sat himself on the palace door of Gopīcānd. There, the music did not have tune any more. Horses and elephants did not eat, little babies did not suck milk. Then the king recognized that these were due to the power of the ācārya, and being overcome, he spent a little in alms and invited the ācārya and his followers to dinner. As the ācārya said that he had four times hundred thousand men with him, he could not possibly satiate them; but the king answered that when he was in a position to supply constantly the food of many ten thousands of soldiers, why could he not feed the ācārya and his followers. Thereupon, the ācārya said. 'I have two disciples: Mahila and Bhadali, first you feed them with satisfaction.' Following this conversation, the king had rice cooked for five hundred people. Then came both Mahila and Bhadali, poured the whole food in a gourd made into two shells (Kamaṇḍalu ?), and as it was not filled the king was surprised. Therefore, the king went to the ācārya and prayed: 'I pray for the means to avoid death.' Then the ācārya received all belongings for Maṇḍala and he gave Abhiṣeka to the king. And as he gave him the same lesson as the former street-sweeper, the king said that he had heard all these before and narrated to him the former affair. Thereupon, the ācārya said: 'How can you now acquire Siddhi to avoid death as this one was my teacher Jalandhari'? 'Out of fear that he would get a curse from the Siddha' the king begged of the ācārya to find out a means. Three statues of the king were made of copper mixed with eight precious metals. Then Kṛṣṇacāri and his disciples removed all dirt, earth etc.

and brought a statue of the king on the edge of the hole and put it on the feet of the Siddha Hāḍi. Then came out of the mouth of the Guru the words: 'Who art thou?' and the answer came: 'I am king Gopācandra', the Guru said: "Thou art the carcase for a jackal to make multure, become dust', and the figure fell down as dust."

The other statues underwent the same fate.—(Translator).

"Thereupon the hearts of the king and his followers were almost broken. Again, came the ācārya to the king and induced him to apologize. Then came a word from Siddha Jalandhari : 'Mine son Kāhṇa, thou willst take him as thine disciple', but as this one put himself before the ācārya, already one thousand four hundreds were there, the ācārya said : 'You are there, therewith I have innumerable grand-children, but as I have not eaten and drunk for twelve years, I am hungry and thirsty, in the meantime when the dinner will be ready, two must take care of me as I bathe.' In the meantime the seventy new disciples prepared the bath and others were allowed to leave the bath, and as only Dhamma and Dhuma remained, they were asked to attend Jalandhari ; there he cut with a curved knife the flesh from the limbs of them and entwined it in his body. As they said : 'As the Guru has wished it, he is making himself strong with it.' Then broke out the Siddha Jalandhari into endless laughter : 'Hā, Hā ! as I hold fast to my vow, wherefore I eat human flesh ?' Then all disappeared as an illusion of the eyes. As both Dhamma and Dhuma had put their hands on their heads, they acquired the highest Siddhi. As the king and the ācārya were for a long time together as disciple and teacher all the spots were gradually cleansed from the king's character. After the end of six months Gaṅacakra Jalandhari taught Dohā-songs to the king and as the king lived in peace of soul with a thousand following, he became a greater Yogī. The king Bhartāhari was the uncle of the king Gopīcandra.

Further at a later period in a wood near Rāmeśvara in the south was a self-made shrine of the Mātṛkās. There assembled many Dākinīs and Piśācas who used to fall upon all people who came to the south in that road. Once five hundred merchants and a Yogī travelled in this region ; some Brāhmaṇs with their wives put themselves up there and said : 'As you must stay here in the woods, there is an abundance of trees and roots ; besides, there is nothing to fear from the wild beasts.' As these people put up themselves there, two strange women appeared and said : 'You remain here ? You do not know what will put (come) in here ? Answering that they do not know, they said : 'These are the Dākinīs and Rākṣasas, you will be bound by them ; they would come to eat you up tonight, therefore think of remedy against it.'

The accompanying Yogī belonged to the school of Jalandhari ; this one directed his prayer to his ācārya Jalandhari, and there he (Jalandhari) put himself up as a monastery steward in the first watch of the night without saying a word to the Yogī. In midnight appeared the man-eating Dākinīs and Rākṣasas, everyone bound the body of a man and taking him away, put him before the shrine of the Mātṛkās, and made themselves ready to devour them. But as the monastery steward uttered the word : '*Phat*' (फट्) and made dancing movements, the Dākinīs and Rākṣasas became senseless and fell to the ground. The shrine of the Mātṛkās fell down into three pieces. The ācārya gave them the order not to injure any living being any longer; then it followed that the steward was the Siddha Jalandhari himself. And the five hundred merchants became Yogīs and meditated and all acquired the Siddhi. Thus it is narrated. The ācārya stayed in the south for three years and worked for the salvation of living creatures. And it is evident that there were a lot of Upadeśas which he gave at that time.

Again, at another time there lived in the western country of Maru an ācārya named Jñānagupta. As he once was preaching a great sermon, there came in a wonderful Yogī at that time. In answer to the question who he was, he said that he was Jalandhari. After religious discourses Jalandhari gave him a skull-cup full of light. Ācārya Jñānagupta took it without consideration and at the same time extinguished the light. As the members of the Saṅgha repeatedly prayed him to remain, he gave Upadeśas for three months to them. Finally he told them : 'Keep everything in the secrecy of your memory for three years, after that bring all the Tantra powers to function and you according to your wish will have holy life ! And all will acquire the Siddhis.' Saying this he became invisible. Once in the eastern country he received the cry from six Yogīs : 'Jalandhari come here and teach us the Dhamma !' As they went to the temple, ācārya indeed came, but he did not show himself up there.

After they had built a prayer-house and prayed there, he showed his face six months later and gave them essential instructions. In the course of a week there came a Saindhava-Śrāvaka. He is said to have told him: 'You shall learn nothing of *Tattva*, he who rejoices himself on some dialectic has became an inveterate Bhiksu and to him it has became old' and he disappeared. In this cloister now came many Saindhava-Śrāvakas and lived there. The six Yogīs received the Siddhi of immortality. The oldest of them seemed to have been Vibhūticandra. He came to Tibet and Bu-Ston-Rin-Po-Che prayed him for instruction. Now, the ācārya appeared in the world for four times. Among the disciples of the teacher, the first place belonged to Kṛṣṇacāri, the second Buddhajñanapāda, besides Mahāsiddha Tānti, the younger Virūpa, the kings Bhartāhari and Gopicandra etc. Under these circumstances, who was the best disciple, the prophesy said that he could carry the name 'Black'; he would consequently after Khatvaṅga (Śatavaṅga) follow Kālacakra, and carried ornaments of bones and a Damaru in the form of a brandy-glass. (pp. 58-69).

As regards the life-history of Kṛṣṇacāri the tradition of the old Tibetans is that he was born in the country of Karṇa, while the oral tradition that exists amongst the present day Indian Yogīs is that he was born in the city of Pādyanagara which is also called Vidyānagara (Vijayanagara). When it is narrated that he was of the Brāhmaṇa caste that agrees with the old tradition of the Indians, and when the old Tibetans say that he was of Ārya family that accords with the Dohā of the ācārya himself : 'Wrestling and striving forward-going is the son of the Brāhmaṇa.' Thus he was a man who shining in the Brāhmaṇa-caste, advanced the aim of the Bauddhas, but remained outwardly harmonizing with the heterodox people. There existed already a prophesy from Buddha for the country of Uruvica, which according to my Guru meant Odivica, which touches Bengal, and this prophesy refers to the appearance of Kṛṣṇacāri. According to the translation of Śesrab from Rva-Sgren, which reports freely over the manifestations of the Nātha, this identity with Odivica is evident. The son born there will be provided with great bravery and when promoted to the order of Rāmana will receive all Siddhantra, as the only Yogeśvara will carry a name, which touches a little on N to the fourth (consonant) of the seventh line, provided with the first vocal with first (consonant) of the first line. He did not appear in Jambudvīpa, therefore he will not appear here also. His six disciples will throw away the existence of their bodies and attain Mahāmudrāsiddhi.' Thus, his motherland, his name, his Siddhi and his disciples were previously pointed out. As regards the life-history of this ācārya, one should examine the especially published *r Nam-t'ar*. The six of the disciples of this ācārya prophesied by Buddha were : Bhadrapāda, Mahila, Bhadala, the Cramaneṛa called Tailor, Dhamma and Dhuma. Others say that Bhadala, Bhadra or Bhadrapāda were identical and do not count him separately ; in his place they take Eyalā or also the Yoginī Mekhalā and Kanakhalā or Bandhe etc. At the time when the ācārya lived himself the following persons received the highest Siddhi : minister Kuśalanātha, king Lilācandra further Amitavajra, prince Lavaji and others became indescribable lordly Yogīsvaras and as they met later the Brāhmaṇa Śrīdhara and his followers, they acquired the Siddhi. Ācārya Bhadra gave his teachings to Antara, he to the man who enjoyed the fame to be the younger Kṛṣṇacāri, this to Bhuvari, this one to Tibetan-born Bhuva bLo-ldan and he preached to

Kuśalibhadra, thus this was a school. Further, preached Kṛṣnacāri also to Bhadrapāda who was famous under the name of Guhya. He must have preached to ācārya Tilli. In Tibet they say that the above-mentioned Guhya (Bhadrapāda) preached to Anṭara, and this one to Tilli.

This Mimāṅsaka preached also to Kuśalanātha. As this one gave up the post of a minister, meditated and gained somewhat clairvoyance power. (pp. 69-72).

As regards ācārya Tilli, he was born in the Brāhmana caste in the eastern city of Caṭighavo, when he grew up, he learnt all the text-books of the Brāhmaṇa religion, while wandering as a mendicant, he came finally to a temple-monastery and seeing the members of the Sangha leading an unattached life, he became a believer, put on the monk's robes and learnt the *Tripitaka*. He received the Abhiṣeka to Maṇḍalas, grasped the Upadeśas etc., meditated and became participant of all knowledge. He saw the immeasurable face of Magic-Puruṣa. He also saw constantly the face of Śrīherukā and of the Dākinīgaṇas. As he united himself with a maiden Yoginī of his Kṣetra who pounded sesame, he was driven out of the cloister by the members of the Saṅgha. Then, he busied himself with the pounding of sesame in the city, and as he, a former Brāhmaṇa-Paṇḍita Bhikṣu did not succeed to became a man of honour and rank, he received the name Tilli, i.e. who pounds sesame, and he was the husband of such a woman. After he had worked in different Kṣetras, he received all instructions from the Dākinīs of the countries beginning from Udayāna. As he now pushed the teachings of his Guru bodily also to the highest point, he succeeded in getting the knowledge of Sahajavidyā by experience, and thus reached the highest Siddhi. With the intention of showing his knowledge to others, once he sung the songs of his knowledge to the assembled people of the market of the city. All men were in doubt when once in a city of Bengal assembled hundred thousand men to see him, the ācārya appeared with the Śakti pounding Śesamc in the air above the ground about a man's height. And as people asked him different questions, he gave answers in a song of his experience. It is narrated that the assembled people understood the sense and acquired the Siddhi. Thus he became famous as Siddha Tilli. After working for the salvation of all creatures for a long time, he went bodily to heaven. (pp. 72-73).

His disciples were Lalitavajra and Nāro. A report on the first person does not exist. It is clear that what appeared *Maitriyogīdharmacakra* (मैत्रीयोगीधर्म्मचक्र) is connected with him and in the legend of the younger Lotsaba-collection of Mar-do and Pu-rang on Sambara and in the legend on Hevajra from dPyal, he as a Gautama-Śiṣya was made as the best disciple. (pp. 73-74).

As regards Nāro, he was born in a Brāhmana family in Kāśmira. As in his youth he was a Tirthika-Paṇḍita, he practised all the Tantras of the Tirthikās. As an ascetic of the Brāhmaṇa caste he made Avadhūti. Once, he came in the house of a brandy-sȩlling woman where there was an unimportant Bauddha-Paṇdita. This one could not bear the magnificence of Nāro, and he ran away from there. As Nāro found there the beginning work of a *Sūtra*-copy he rejoiced himself very much on the religion of the Buddhas. Then, he went to Madyadeśa, declared himself for the teaching of the Bauddhas and became a greater Paṇḍita. Then he became the northern door-keeper of Nalanda and Vikramaśilā. Later, to enfeeble the Tirthikas he delivered many sermons and afterwards meditated on Cakrasamvara. During this time when a large number of Dākinīs showȩd him their faces he received the exhortation. 'Go to Tilli, who now dwells in the east, there you will acquire the Siddhi."

After a miraculous meeting Nāro met Tilli and became his disciple.—(Translator).

"But he having nearly violated the order of the teacher, did not attain the highest Siddhi in his lifetime. He died a natural death. (pp. 74-78).

As regards the disciples of this ācārya they were the door-keepers: Paṇḍita as Śānti, experienced in disputes; superior Atīśa and also other disciples for uncommon things—of them four were acquainted with the preached Dhāraṇis for the Pitṛ-Tantras, and four for the Mātṛ-Tantras. The first four were: Kṛṣṇābhayavajra, Pi-to-ha-nu, Jayākara, the Kāśmīri Ākarasiddhi; the second four: Manakaśrī, Dharmamati, the great Guru from P'am-tin and Prajñārakṣita. Thus they were people who had acquired magic-powers. Some count Pi-to-ha-nu and Dharmamati to be the same person, whereby Jñānagarbha comes in the group of first four. Again, there were other four disciples who had acquired magic-powers: Śrīdombi, Riri, Kānta and Kasori; these all had acquired the Siddhi. (pp. 78-79).

Śrīdombi was originally a shepherd, keeping a flock of cattle of a king. He had no schooling. He got the Abhiṣeka to Hevajra-Maṇḍala from Nāro. Once during swimming he was eaten up by a fish, but having meditated the Maṇḍala of Herukā he came out without any harm. As it appeared to him to be necessary to write many text-books, he now entered schools and refuted the criticism of the Tirthikas and Bauddha-Paṇditas through words of Dharma The neighbouring world was filled with his fame. He was Atīśa's Guru. As regards his personal collaboration with Atiśa, according to the Tibetans, Śrīdombi put down the true and unchangeable sense in four texts-books with commentary from Atīśa. I myself have seen in the hands of my teacher Nirguṇa a Sanskrit-copy divided into chapters which harmonizes with that of the Indian savant. (pp. 79-80).

The youngest Kuśalibhadra prayingly solicited for discipleship to the ācārya Dobmi the younger. This ācārya was born in Mewar which is in western India. From his youth he knew many Vedas. As he prayed to a great Tirthika-teacher that he might convert (take him to discipleship) him, this one declined it.

As he conceived that he must criticise the Tirthikas he went to Vajrāsana, (Bodh-Gayā) became a monk and studied and knew all the *Pitakas*. Later, dressed as a Brāhmaṇa he went to Kāmaru (Kāmarūpa), studied with at least six Brāhmaṇas and Tirthikas all their magic-books and he was trusted by them. Then he appropriated to himself all the magic-tricks of Kāmaru, many Tantras of Vijigiri sect, many had Tantras of the Dākinīs, and many methods of exorcism of Syannari and he practised them. Then he returned to the above Tirthika-Paṇdita. There was king Karṇa who gathered two thousands of Bauddha Yogīs and Paṇditas and eight thousands of Tirthikas and held a discussion. Then came the disputes. A Tirthika Yogī let two meteors fall from heaven. Both were black, and in the shapes of houses but with human heads. Ācārya knowing these to be eye-illusions muttered Dhāraṇīs to annul them and both of them transformed themselves into little pieces of coals ; then some of the Tirthikas showed a piece of art—as flames from the fire coming out of the body. But he put water on it and extinguished the fire. Thus all the attacks were parried each time and juggling works were defeated by the juggling works. In the end, the four leading teachers of the Tirthikas, were transformed into cats by the magic-power of the ācārya. Now the Buddhists increased very much in this country.

But he knowing this to be unreal and jugglery, became an a-begging Yogī and applied himself to Śrīdombi. He was given the Abhiṣeka with the Maṇdala of Sambara and Hevajra. Then he went to Devikote in the east and meditated without food and drinking only water; a Bhūt (an evil spirit) was his servant. (pp. 80-83).

His disciple was Asitaghana. He was originally a Tirthika Yogī and was born in Prayāga. He got from god Maheśvara enchanted quicksilver. As he practised his jugglery on an a-begging Yogī, he lost his magic-powers of quicksilver; then he became a believer of Buddha and applied himself to Paṇdita Prabhavarman, Mahācārya Ratnarakṣita, Vibhūticandra, Devakara and other Upadeśakas. He mastered Tantras and collections over Sambara, Hevajra, Bhairava and four thrones. He lived two hundred years. He wrote small books on Tantra and he taught Jñānamitra. (pp. 83-84).

Jñānamitra was a low caste man from Tripurā. He became a monk of Jagaddali; then he became a much respected head of monastery. The Vinaya was his method, also he knew the *Abhidharmapitaka*; he understood well the text of Mahāyāna; further, he had many ācāryas with him who were especially entrusted with the Guhyā-Tantras; he learned profoundly the collections on Yamāntaka, Sambara and Hevajra, Guhya-Candratilaka, Mahāpāṇitilaka and the Kālacakra. He belonged also to the succession of the school of Dharma and with him was one who was also an a-begging monk, he prayed on 'four thrones' and Mahāmāyā. As he meditated on these teachings, he met Siddha Asitāghana. This one gave him the Upadeśas on the three Inspirations. As he became completely gifted with the knowledge of *Sampannakrama* and as he stood praying, the Guru said: "Now in twelve years an ācārya with Gnana endowment will come to Candradvīpa, go a-begging with my Upadeśas, take my Upadeśas as basis, then you will acquire the Mahāmudrā-siddhi." With the words: 'Go to Udayāna' went up magically the ācārya in heaven. Then, in the middle of twelve years he became a man of sublime spiritual acquisition. With the idea that he must be active as the preponderance of the Tirthikas may harm the religion, he withdrew himself from it. As he wanted to go to Candradvīpa emerged up ācārya Nandapāla from the earth by the door of benediction. He came to this Dvīpa (island) and met him. Then he prayed to him for the four Mudrā-Upadeśas. On an occasion of the other three Mudrās Nandapāla preached to him the Upadeśa: 'I see myself great in spirit' and thereupon the Mahāmudrā that he saw on the Vidyādhara-body of this Guru, annulled all doubts and he reached the ground of all Dharmas.

He disappeared again through the door of benediction of ācārya Nandapāla and emerged up in two and a half hundred years in the south. There he met ācārya Asitaghana. This one was on the border of his second hundredth year when he met the ācārya. Thereupon began the ācārya to work with activity.

Once he was in Odivisa (Orissā) country where is the self-built stone image of the god Viṣṇu in the Tırthika-temple named Jagannātha, which is extremely rich in miracles. There the ācārya sat at the foot of the door with four Yoginīs and asked for entry to the Castellan. As this one spoke with a Tirthika Guru who said he would be fit to be the master of the temple, the Castellan answered it is doubtless that 'This Bauddha does not believe in all our gods, but it appears that he is a house-holder Āryā, he may be allowed to visit knowing that he has before him the god of the country.' Then the ācārya entered the temple and stood long in respectful position. Then the Castellan smote him with a baton. The ācārya blew a horn, thereby the stone statues of the temple of Jagannātha lost their extremities and organs and their former wonder powers. As there was no member of the old Buddhist convents there was a new spreading of Buddhism in the course of hundred years while three kings reigned. Even now there are few Bauddhas. He acquired the Śūṇyatā (शून्यता). Finally, he acquired the highest Siddhi. Ācārya Dharmakara who acquired the rainbow-body in Āmradvīpa, the Yoginī Candraprabhā and the Yoginī Bhaja duru were his three older disciples and later Mahāsiddha Śāntigupta the fourth disciple. Here closes the fifth chapter on the combined narration of four Inspirations" (Pp. 88).

INSPIRATION V

The fifth Inspiration follows now:
In Madhyadeśa in the district of Khabi was the city of Takśaśila (Tavilā). There was a Brāhmana ācārya, who became a monk in Nālāndā of Mahāsāṅghika school and received the name of Buddhaśrījñāna. Some say, he was of Kṣatriya caste and reader to the king. He learned Mahāyāna and Hīnayāna *Pitakas*, texts and commentaries with ācārya Siṅhabhadra, and as one Guṇamitra asked him, he wrote many text-books, especially a complicated commentary on *Prajñāpāramitā*-tradition, and on scrutiny of the commentary it is proved that he was no Bhiksu.

As Buddhaśrijñāna went to the west towards Udayāna he discussed with ācārya Līlāvajra and Yoginī Guṇeru about many heterodox and Budhist Dhāraṇī-learnings. In the north of Udayāna there was a Caṇḍāla girl by the name of Jatijālā. With this holy queen for eight months he gave himself up to some Tantras and as he had received a prophesy from Jambala, he got Vidyā-Tantra immediately with it. (pp. 87-89).

As regards the history of offerings at Vajrāsana, it is thus: As once the ācārya set in his hut which he had built near Vajrāsana, there came king Dharmapāla to give alms to Vajrāsana. All the Bauddha-ācāryas came to the gift. As he saw the ācārya not taking part in it, the king thought that he wanted to humilate him. Now as he entered the hut of the ācārya, he saw that the ācārya was not there, but a statue of Mañjusrī. Then he looked around and asked his companions. With their answer: 'But he is here' he re-entered and the ācārya became visible. Then followed a miracle.—(Translator).

"The king became a believer and prayed for Abhiṣeka and as he had no more gift to give, bound himself and his wife to be his servants; in the meantime he brought gold from his palace as high as his stature and that of his wife as ranson money. (p. 92).

Here follows the history of the consecration of Vikramasila:

There were four temple-monasteries, these were separated by spaces covering distances of many days. Now as regards Vikramaśilā, it was newly built, Somapurī restored, and while many new temple-buildings were in the course of construction, the king ordered their consecration. There appeared the ācārya magically doubling his body four times and consecrating simultaneously all four temples. The Tirthikas came to confuse them (inmates of the convents), but they were defeated by greater exorcism. They came every year even in those days and could do no harm. (pp. 92-93).

History of conversions in Nalanda:

The great ācārya was the president of Nālānda and Vikramaśilā. At that time when the ācārya was dwelling in Nalanda, the Saindhava Śrāvakas in Otantpurī (Odantapurī) who were monks, who had gone astray through doubt and had become degraded and maintained Buddhajñāna without discipline and hence declared as unbecoming and improper for the abbot of the Sangha and as having disgraced the Tantras. In Vajrasana, many Saindhava and Siṅghala-Bhikṣus destroyed the silver-moulded image of Herukā and made profit out of it. And for that reason the king[1] killed many of the Siṅghala Bhikṣus, but the great ācārya out of his great mercy sheltered them from their extinction by the king. He (ācārya) lived for more than eighty years. (pp. 93-94).

He had eighteen disciples, the prominent of them were: Dipaṅkara-Śrībhadra, Prasānta-

(1) The king must have been Dharmapāla.—(Translator).

mitra Mahāsukha, Padmakara and Kṣatriya Rāhula. (p. 94).

Dipaṅkarabhadra was born in western India. After learning the Vedas, he became later either a monk of a temple-monastry or the president of Mahāsāṅghika Sangha. He met the great ācārya Buddhajñāna in Nālandā. He was killed by a Tirthika king in Sindhu who always used to harm the disciples of the ācārya. Some histories mention him as the Turuska king Bhūṣaṇa, but there were no Turuskas in Madhyadeśa at that time. (pp. 95-96).

In Mālwa the Tirthika king worshipped Mahāviṣṇu and destroyed many temples of the Buddhists. He drove out the Bhikṣus from Madhyadeśa and injured the Upāsakas. The ācārya worked exorcism, the king and the queen fell sick and the king died. The threatening minister was made cold by Dhāranis. (pp. 96-97).

Sagaracandra was an ācārya of the Tirthikas. He practised exorcism of the Hexen and damaged the Bauddhas. One day he met the ācārya in a street and said: 'If you do not die tomorrow morning, then our religion is false' and made exorcism. But the Tirthika died at midnight. (p. 97).

Vaidyāpāda was a disciple of this ācārya.

He was a Brāhmana, born in a frontier place. He needed a Candāla girl (चण्डालिनी) for the support of his magic, and got one by giving her parents gold procured miraculously as high as her stature. He reached the highest state of Mahāmudrā-siddhi. After he had written many text-books, bodily he flew up to the heaven like a Garuṛa-prince to the Kṣetra of the Buddha-Akṣobhya.

Ācārya Huṅkara, as mentioned in rNin-mapa, was identical with him. If it be so, then Nepāl should be his birth-place and people know that he came to Tibet in the time of king Sad-na-legs.

Ācārya Avadhūti got instruction from him; from him Ratnākara Śānti, from him Vājrāsana the senior. Further, from him Kuśali and thus it is said was a succession. Further, when Vaidyāpāda became the prince of Inspirations the Udayāna-ācārya Buddhaśrīśānti prostrating himself prayed to him; from him again Vajrāsana the big, from him either Vajrāsana from the country of Sauri or also Ratnākaragupta and Vajrāsana the younger. Further, Mahācārya Buddhajñānapada preached to the ācārya Padma-'byuri-gnas. He was also called as the later Padmavajra or the small one. The name 'the big senior and the junior Padma' was related only to their earlier or later appearance.

Ācārya Vaidyapāda taught Avadhūti Yogi Ratnaśīla of Kāmaru. The Kāyastha-Vṛddha or the 'old-writer' of Dharmapāla learnt from him too. He was eighty years old, and became a monk at Nālāndā.

By showing a miracle—(Translator) he became the Guru of king Mahāpāla. This ācārya built many temple-cloisters for the Guhya-Tāntrikas. It was he who wrote the Hevajra-commentary *Suvicadaśamputa* about which, it is said that Taṅkadāsa had written it. But as in this commentary 'the former foolish Yogī' prayed, therefore, according to the inscription-page of the translation of Glan-Dharmamati, the author would be the Kāyastha-Vṛddha. In the translation of bLo-brtan of Son, the composition-element contained, the name of the one and the same ācārya. As regards the commentry, it is considered that it might have been written by a disciple in succession of teaching of this ācārya, which in this case ācārya Bhāvaskandha would be understood. (pp. 97-100).

This ācārya taught Durhari, this one to the former Vajrāsana. The younger Vajrāsana prayed for instruction from him. Now as regards Mahāvajrāsana he was born in the country of Mālwa. He completed the Veda-schooling of the Brāhmaṇa caste, later he became a monk in Nālāndā. Also, he knew profoundly all the Brāhmaṇas and Bauddha-Tantras; he was great especially in Upadeśas. At the time, when Atiśa appeared, he exercised his power as the abbot of Vajrāsana, later he became also the abbot of Vikramaśilā. His disciple was Vajrāsana the younger or Ratnākaragupta. (pp. 100-101).

This one was born in the eastern country of Gauṛa in the Brāhmaṇa caste. From his youth he knew the *Sutras* and Tantras profoundly, took five vows on himself, and took Vajrāsana as his ācārya, but he remained as a believing Upāsaka. As many Bhikṣus crossed the country and preached in Madhyadeśa, a believing minister of a king told him that he might become a Bhikṣu, otherwise the religion would be injured when *Tripiṭaka*-holding Bhikṣu would be denied by a Upāsaka. Thereupon he answered that he had got to support an old mother, as a Bhikṣu he could not do it; then the minister gave him sixty gold coins for the support of his mother. Then he became a monk in Vikramaśilā. Therewith the Upadeśas of the Paṇḍita and Yogī reached a high degree. Later on, the ācārya in consideration of his great heart remained in Sauri, thereupon he received the name of 'the man from Sauri.'

Subsequently, he reached the goal of the *Utpattikrama*, viewed the faces of many protecting gods and made the Upadeśas very successful in the country of India. The Upadeśas he gave to the ācārya Abhayākara, this one to Śubhākaragupta, this one to Daśabala, this one to Yogī Vajraśrī. This one to Dharmabhadraśrī famous as the most clever amongst all the ācāryas in the case of disputes; this one to Buddhakīrti, this one to Ratnakīrti, this one to Ratigupta. For a long time, legends of the above-mentioned persons, were not handed down.

Here closes from the history which is compared to 'a Mine of Precious Stones' the sixth chapter of the presentation of *Utpattikrama*-tradition. (pp. 101-102).

INSPIRATION VI

"As regards the sixth Inspiration which refers to the tradition of the texts, therewith the Tāntrikas were meant who explained the Tantras when they represented the tradition of the texts.

It was a difficult task with Nāro and Maitri to comment on a great mass of Tantras, some had been delivered by Nāgārjuna to Ārya-deva, who to Rāhula, and he to Candrakīrti, who to Prabhākara, and this one to Jñāna-śakti, and he to Śānti.

Further, lots of Tantra-commentaries had been handed over by Mañjuśrīmitra to Brāhmaṇa Jñānavajra, and this traditional materials with that of Bodhivajra-Śrijñāna-pāda were subsequently transferred to Pra-śantamitra.

The latter taught four disciples: Śrīsena, Śilu, Kṛṣṇajāta Vaidyāpāda. Mañjuśrī-jñāna learnt with the latter, from him the great Amoghavajra, Siddhivīra with the latter, from him Atiśa; Mitraguhya also sought teaching of him. (pp. 103-104).

While the series ran further their number became larger. In opposition to them, ācārya Lalitavajra brought a large number of Tantras from Udayāna and delivered them to ācārya Līlāvajra. This one delivered them to Mañjuśrījñāna. Also the ascetic and Brāhmaṇa ācārya Śrīdhara acquired the Mahāmudrāsiddhi. He was a good-lecturing and *Tripitaka*-knowing Bhikṣu of Vidharbha in the southern country. He was threatened by a Tirthika king who wanted to break his head. His head was cut off, but he put on a buffalo-head on his shoulders. He went to Harikela to preach. There exorcised a cat, hence he was called Bhiradi or Birālī. (p. 104).

Further, there were some Tantras written by Kukuri. He was born in the east in the country of Bengal. He became a Bhikṣu-Paṇdita in Nalanda."

A miraculous story is narrated here,—(Translator).

"He lived with Vajrayoginī who looked like a she-dog before the world. Hence he was called Kukuri. This ācārya took, as a Yogī of Śrīvajrabhairava, the pose of a destroyer, and there was a history that a king of the Tajiks (Persian) with his elephants were reduced to dust. He was the same person who gave teaching to Amonghavajra. (p. 104). He brought many Tantras from the world of the Dākinīs and taught them to Padmavajra, this one to Tilli, this one to Nāro, and this one to Śānti. (p. 105).

Śānti was born of Brāhmaṇa caste in Magadha. He studied profoundly the Vedas and the Vedāngas from his youth. Some say that he was a Ksatriya. He became a monk in Otantapuri, comprehended in his spirit the whole *Tripitakas* of the Srāvakas, then he went to Vikramaśilā, heard many Mahāyāna-Sutras and text-books with many learned men as the great Jetari, and became a great Sthavira-ācārya. He was ordained as the abbot of Somapuri and stayed there for many years. There he attached himself to many Gurus viz. Ratnakīrti, Kālasamayavajra Thagana and heard hundred Tantras and impressed them upon his spirit. Then he went to Mālwa where he observed a vow for seven years, finally he saw the face of Mañjughoṣa, Tārā and Ajitanātha (Maitreya) and enjoyed the Amṛta (nectar) of the holy religion. The ācārya received in dream the order of Ārya-Tārā. 'Go to Siṁhaladvīpa', and the king of Sinhala also received the order in dream: "In Jambudvipa there is an ācārya Ratnākaraśānti, bring him here, he shall spread Mahāyāna (doctrine) in thy country." At the same time the ācārya and the messenger of the king came to Bengal. He brought two hundred *Mahāvānasūtras* with him and preached for seven years in Sinhala. There arose five hundred Mahāyāna Saṅghas, and the Sūtra-schools spread extra-ordinarily. When it is also sure that old Siṅhala had given many Siddhas, so it is clear that still there were Śrāvaka-Saṅghas.

On his way back to Jambudvīpa the sea became stormy and thieves came there. Muttering the Dhāraṇīs he threw down a handful of sand offering, brought the robbers and thieves in his power and the sea became calm. Then he passed through some countries of south India and reached Vajrāsana (Bodh-Gayā). As the ācārya came in the morning, the king prayed him to stay in Vikramaśilā. That time, he became the eastern door-keeper of Vikramaśilā. In some histories it is said, that this king was Mohipāla, in others it is said that this was his relative king Canaka. Of these two views the last must be correct.

There, sooner or later he fought with two hundred Tirthika-Paṇḍitas and overcame them ; his fame spread in all countries. He had no rival amongst the Bauddhas, he was respected as the Guru of the king. In the time of a dispute he received the by-name Sarvajña. After becoming hundred and eight years old, he left the body As his disciples were busy in burning his dead body in Citavaha, the body became invisible as soon as fire was lighted. (pp. 105-109).

Further there was the king Indrabhūti the junior. In the name of Kukurarāja he preached Dharma in the day to a thousand dogs and in the night he lived thoroughly according to his vows. It is sure that many Tantras were received from him, and he taught some of them as ācārya Padma'byuri prayed for it, but these texts are no longer in use. And many books that will be narrated in the history of Atīśa, have not been preserved. (p. 109).

There are a large number of Tāntrik-books of Kālacakra and books connected with it. Pito received a commission from Vajrāpāṇi, to acquire virtue, went to Cambhala magically, brought many Tantras with him and in Ratnagiri taught many students. Pito himself acquired first the Siddhi of invisibility. Out of his six disciples, three received Vajra-body and became invisible. Bhiksu Avadhūti, Bodhiśrī and Nāro propagated further. Thus, Avadhūti delivered to Sauri. To him Pito, who came in the time of king Mahīpāla, gave up the superiority of the Tantras of Abhiyuktakas and all their whole tradition. Thus, the whole tradition of the learned texts of the different Gurus came in the possession of the great ācārya, the Buddha of the setting time Abhayākaragupta. (p. 109).

Ācārya Abhayākaragupta was born in Jarikhanda, which lies near to the country of Odivisa in the south. His father was a Kṣatriya, his mother a Brāhmaṇī. From his youth he was well-read in the Vedas and Vedāṅgas, well-built in language and dialectic ; as adult, he learnt all the text-books and Tantras of the Tirthikas. As he sat in a garden uttering Tantras, there sat a beautiful maiden by his side. She said : 'I am a Chaṇdāla-maiden, and would like to remain with you.' But he said : 'How that can be possible ? I belong to a higher caste, it would be a dishonour to me.' Therewith he obtained vision that she had disappeared. Then he understood that she could be only a godddess or Yakṣiṇī, therefore he asked his brother of the order, a Bauddha Yogī. He said : 'That is Vajrayoginī and it is not good that you have not taken the Siddhi from her ; you are destined to the religion of the Bauddhas, go to the east and become a Bauddha.' And he did that accordingly. He studied in Bengal to become versed in all the Sūtra-Tantras and he prayed to many ācāryas for the Abhiṣeka.

As he became a great *Pitaka*-knowing person, he became famous as ācārya of all Vinaya-dharas.

Once, as he was sitting in the court of a temple cloister, there appeared a young maiden who dragged on a piece of beef near to him which was dripping in blood, shoved it to the ācārya and said: 'I am a Candāla-maiden, but eat what is slaughtered for you.' But he answered: 'I am a Bhikṣu of purer order, how shall I eat meat which is extraordinarily offered to me ? But she sank back and disappeared in the court below. That was again Vajrayoginī who gave him the Siddhi, but he did not take it. In order to learn further, he stayed at Nalanda."

Later when Vajrayoginī told him that thrice she offered him the Siddhi and he did not receive it, the best he had not acquired in his life. Now he should write books, teach the Dharma and before death would reach the highest.—(Translator).

"From there he began to wander in different burning-places (Śaśmāna) to meditate, but as the wife of the king Rāmapāla built and presented the temple-cloister of Edapura, he dwelt there in contemplation."

After performing some miraculous acts—(Translator), "he became the abbot of Vajrasana. Later, he became the abbot of Nalanda and Vikramaśilā and the king honoured him as his Guru. Induced by the prayers of his disciples he began to write the commentary on *Prajñapāramitā* containing the eight thousand verses (अष्टसाहस्रिका·प्रज्ञापारमिता) As he worked on three Māla-divisions of Vajrāvalināmamaṇḍala, fell a shower of flowers-rain, and in the time when he worked on the *Upadeśamanjarī*, Sambara, Hevajra and Kālacakra who lived in three highest regions, glorified him in bliss, and his fame and glory filled all the world. Besides these, he wrote the *Śākyamatālaṅkāra* for the *Prajñāpāramitā*, the *Lokasaṅkṣepa* for the *Abhidharma*, the *Bhikṣuvidyātīkā* for the *Vinaya* with the explanation of the *Vinaya* the *Madhyamamanjurī* for the Madhyama-teaching ; for the Yoga and for these Tantras no commentaries were present. He made some *Tīkās*: the four famous books of exorcism-methods, the *Buddhakpālatīka*, commentaries of many Matṛka-Tantras in the form of a Sūtra of *Abhayamārgakrama*, the *Pancakramatīkā*, the *Ganavatāra* and commentaries on and explanations to Kālacakra. He wrote also many small text-books and gave many subtle, innumerable exorcism-methods, and arranged the compilations of different exorcism-methods.

In India and in Tibet there are large numbers of his disciples. All the Indian teachers of Mahāyāna who came after him, openly accepted him as the standard, and so did Śubhakaragupta. He taught Daśabala, and Daśabala taught Vikrtideva. (pp. 109-114).

Vikṛtideva was a well-informed Bengali-Paṇdita. He went to Nalanda and busied himself much about Dharma and all the Upadeśas. Though, when he left his motherland, he promised his original Guru to be a monk, he did it later, but as he had desire of the flesh, took a wife and had three children: One boy and two girls. But in dream Avalokiteśvara said as he had broken the order of his Guru, he would die within three years of an infectious disease and would go to hell, he got very much frightened, cut himself off from his family and took vows. But the prophesy was fulfilled, after threo years he got the contagion and died. There his ācārya saw in his mind, how he was taken away by the beadles of the Yama, but five gods and Hayagrīva with Āryāvalokiteśvara at their head struck the hell-beadles and Aryāvalokiteśvara shed tears and ran towards him to bring his body back. And while he was brought back visibly to the Parivāra of the Ārya, he came back to life again. As he had seen the face of Avalokiteśvara, he had greater power, gained success in his spiritiual dignity and the Siddhi.

He taught the Kaśhmira-Pandita Śākyaśrībhadra, Buddhaśrībhadra, Ratnarakṣita. Muniśrībhadra prayed to him ; so also Karuṇāśrībhadra for teaching. This one taught Sākyaraksita, this one to Sujātavarman, this one to Kimpıla Paṇdita Muktadeva, this one to Jñānagupta, this one to Ratigupta, this one to Śantigupta who was free of rivals in this present-day world. (pp. 114-115).

Here closes from the history, which is a equal to a 'Mine of Precious Stones' the seventh chapter, which narrates the origin of the Tantra-commentaries." (p. 115).

INSPIRATION VII

"Now in the eighth chapter follows the Inspiration of various sorts of individual Upadeśas. The Mahāsiddha Gorakṣa-Inspiration of the Upadeśas concerns the narration of the Yogīs of twelve schools. Mina had held himself to Maheśvaradeva, acquired lower Siddhis from him, got the Upadeśas of the highest step of breathing exercises(प्राणायाम) prayed to Gorakṣa, and then meditated. He advanced further as he entered the self-growing Jñāna of Mahāmudrā.

As there are lots of such and unfounded histories, some are here omitted. What is narrated of such things, the authority like the Paṅdita Mahāsiddha-Śāntigupta has not agreed ; same opinion held by our Guru Buddhagupta, who has met personally many Siddhas and is a true treasure of unlimited teachings of Gorakṣa ; while holding as correct the three disciples following Gorakṣa : Tīrthanātha, Kālanātha and Brahmanātha thoroughly harmonize with his claims. (p. 116).

In western India was an ācārya Vyāli. He mixed a large number of drugs together and sought for twelve years long to win Quicksilver-Elixir ; but as there was no sign of success and his materials ran out, he threw the book on Quicksilver-method in the Ganges and went out a-begging. At an opportune moment, when he came to Odivisa, he found the same book while bathing in a river, absolutely unspoiled. He recognized thereby that it was a sign to win the Siddhi, and returned to his mother-country. There the Quicksilver rolled towards the right and a distinguished tune was brought out. As now the members of the house saw a rain of flowers falling, they asked, what was that ? But nobody knew anything about it. Now a somewhat dull-brained girl seemed to have said : 'Here in the room I am strewn over with a powder.' As she was told that she might wash herself, it followed consequently this also : The remark on the uncertainty of the question—what was that, gave rise to introspection ; as he did not know the character of the red Myrobalan, which proved to be the same in the case of the dust fallen on the girl ; he attained at nothing, besides he added a simple red Myrobalan in it, but when blood-drops appeared at the time of washing, the success of the Quicksilver-essence was there. Thereafter, for six months he made an abundance of Quicksilver-preparation. Then Vyāli and his wife, his son and daughter and daughter-in-law ate of it, thus five persons and the sixth creature his horse came in the possession of the ingredients.

As he did not impart the Siddhi to anybody, he sat himself on a big stone and began to think of giving to others the Quicksilver-essence and the stuff of making good, and as he now had acquired the Siddhi, made exorcisms by supporting himself on the Tantras of the Mahākāla.

But ācarya Nāgārjuna heard about it. Nāgārjuna holding himself on the Dhāraṇīs of the 'air-wanderers' (Dākinīs) brought two shoes from the tree-leaves which enabled him to go through the air. The one he concealed he put on the other and flew to Vyāli through the air. As he now demanded that the ācarya must give him the gold-essence, Vyāli answered thereupon: Give me thy shoe, that will be the worth of the gold-essence that I give to you!' Then many Upadeśas for Quicksilver-essence, many hundred thousands, aye many millions of methods of Elixir and beyond it, the power of exorcism to make gold, he gave to Nāgārjuna, and he gave him for it a shoe. Then he put on the hidden shoe and went to India through the air and furthered there very much the Upadeśas of Life-elixir. In the country of Gāndhāra in the north was a mountain called Dhinkota in the district called Munīndra. He wanted to change it into gold and silver, but Āryatārā who knew that would bring the future generations to fight amongst themselves, prevented it and by her blessing changed it to salt. And today it is known by the Gāndhāra country Lati.[1] But Vyāli knowing that his envy had no meaning any longer returned to India. He became bodily a Vidyādhara though he did not have the lowest rank of Bauddha-knowledge ; it was he, to whom the ācārya Carpati who reached the highest Mahāmudrāsiddhi, prayed for the Upadeśa. Vyāli gave Carpati all the Upadeśas of his Elixir of life in the form of a thank-certificate. After this Guru had made a little experiment of Quicksilver-elixir of life, it succeeded at once. As he wanted it to be enjoyed by many beings, he came where there was a large number of nomads. There was a substantially propertied nomad who possessed many thousand buffaloes, buffalo-calves, cattle, horses and sheep. He had provided a wife to his son to whom a small child was born. Occasionally in this neighbourhood there was a festival where the daughter-in-law with her child were present. When the others had gone, the

1. Perhaps the salt-range of western Punjab is meant here.

ācarya came there to beg of his food. She brought all food to him and the ācarya said. 'When thy relatives do not get irritated then give me much food till tomorrow morning, so that you can remain ; but if you are angry, then tarry now while I put fire in the surrounding woods. then fly and come to me !' She took her little child and flew. As she arrived at the place of the ācarya, he gave her the Elixir of life. Thereby she received a Vidyādharī-body and doubled motherhood. Thus she received in quick succession a large number of children. The ācarya gave the Elixir to them also. and there arose three hundred descendants with Vidyādhara-bodies. The king of Campā heard it and the ācarya came with these descendants."

There was a miraculous story in connection with the visit of the ācarya to the king—(Translator). (pp. 116-120).

"His disciple had been the Siddha Kakkuti. When it is said that he received the Brāhmaṇical Abhisekas from the Mahācārya Lui-pā,- yet it is not sure that he lived in the same time with Lui-pā. Later, after receiving the Upadeśas and the connected learning from the Siddha Carpati, he completed the practice in burning-places (Śaśmānas) ; but he went home and became a house-father ; when he came in a town where twelve castes had their seats. He was known as Kukkuṭi. A Kukkutā was not identical with him, there were two persons. (pp. 116-120).

"His disciple was Mina. He was a fisher in the east of India, in Kāmarūpa. As the fisher was in deep contemplation, he had thrown out his angle and drew it, but the fish drew him in its interior and swallowed him. As he was meditating deeply over the power of Karma, he did not die. As the river Rohita[1] that today in Tibetan called gTsan-po, had reached Kāmrūpa, there lay a small hill called Umāgiri, while there Deveśvara zealously gave the Upadeśas to the penitent Umā, and the fish swam in that water. The fisher, lying in the belly of the fish, heard that, meditated over that Upadeśa and had great benefit. As a fisher again caught that fish and killed it, a man was there. Earlier he died there as a king ; thirteen years had just passed that formely a son was born to him. In the belly of the fish he had spent the rest twelve years. Now, the father and the son took themselves to Carpati, prayed for the Upadeśas and performed meditation. And both acquired the Siddhi. The father became famous as the

1. Is it the same as the river Lauhitya which now-a-days is called Brahmaputra?

Siddha Mina, the son as the Siddha Macchindra. The disciples of Siddha Mina were : Hali (a peasant), Māli (a gardener), Tāmbuli (a tooth-painter).[1] These were the three Siddhas. The disciples of Macchindra were Caurangi and Gorakṣanātha. (pp. 120-121). Of these two the first was a son of a King. Once as the king went to another country, the second wife of the king passionately loved the handsome prince. She always waited on the prince, and as he (the prince) did not join in her desire, she became enraged, and as the king came back, she tore off her clothes, put ashes on her head and lay there as if blood would be coming out of her limbs. Then asked the king : 'What has been done to you?' She said : 'That has been done by the son of the king, he came to me to satisfy his desire, and as I did not agree to it, he has thus treated me.' Then without further examinations let the king his guiltless son's arms and legs be cut off and he be thrown in a deep lying place at the foot of a tree in the midst of a much frequented street. Macchindra came there. As the prince narrated his history, this one answered : 'When I am in the position now to furnish you with food, would you be in the

1. Perhaps a mistake is here. In present day Bengal, a Tambuli is a Betel-leaf seller.

position to make twelve years long meditation?' As the prince said that he could do it, there the ācārya Macchindra who himself had a cow-herd as a disciple told this one: 'Under the tree that covers him, lies a man with limbs cut off, furnish him with food for twelve years.' And this one did likewise. After twelve years have passed, at night came many merchants on the street. Caurańgi asked them, who they were. Fearing that he would be the tax-gatherer of the king, they gave out that they were the coal-merchants. Then he said: 'All your wares would be coals.' When the merchants came to the market and put out their wares, all wares have become coals. Then they asked here and there what had passed, and when they considered, thereby they recognized the power of the word of Caurańgi. All the merchants came there, prayed for pardon from Caurańgi and offered him alms. Then said Caurańgi: 'Now all shall again become as before.' As the merchants after going back home saw the wares in their former condition, they now recognised that it had happened through the grace of the ācārya, they wanted to distribute a sacrifice-gift for their life. The ācārya did not accept it, but gave it back to them. And after he had said there: 'Also these limbs may become as before!' this also hap-

r doing all possible good to
and wandering he went up
122).

...kṣa was that cow-herd who
...e food. He had received the
...sa-Yoga of Macchindra ; after performing all outward duties, he meditated and acquired all the magic-skills and Siddhis. Then he reflected that he must give out his spiritual acquisitions to others, and in this matter he gave out his lessons to many men in all countries, and saved them. He made the solemn vow that he would not go to heaven before he had saved ten millions of living beings. And thus he brought the salvation of innumerable men. A complete all-embracing history of this man was not written. As he had doubtless twelve prominent disciples, so the Inspiration had been effective there. (pp. 122-123).

As concerns the Siddha Karṇari, he had been the king in the country of Mewar. Some years had passed that he took a beautiful wife with the name of Piṅgalā. She was very dear to the heart of the king. In order to examine her, once he went alone to a wood and let the false news to be spread, that he had been eaten up by a tiger and thus had met his death. The queen Piṅgalā died from grief, and her dead body was brought to the burning-place. The king did not go back to the city, but stan[illegible] by the side of the dead queen he constan[illegible] wept. 'Alas, alas Piṅgalā!' Thus eight year[illegible] thus twelve years had passed. Then came there Siddha Gorakṣa. Inadvertently he let an earthen vessel (Dipi) fall down from his hand and he broke it. Then he began to lament and remained standing with the complaint: 'Alas alas Dipi.' Then spoke the king: What for this foolish Yogi makes such a lament when his water-vessel is broken?' Then to make it clear that it deals about a stroke that contains an allusion upon the other, spoke the ācrāya: There thou art a fool, as regards my broken pot, it remains to me indeed as my property. Stop your lament over Piṅgalā who is no longer present as she is reduced to dust.' Then he recognized him as the ācārya Gorakṣa and prayed to make him his disciple. He spoke to him: 'Throw away the kingship from you!' As he put away his kingship, he followed him as a disciple. At one time the ācārya ordered that he had got appetite for flesh and spirituous things. As the disciple went to the town to buy flesh and brandy, a woman had exhibited six pieces of pork and six flasks of brandy. She said: 'As price! demand your right eye, I will not be drawn into other bargain.' Then the disciple in order to bring the offering to his ācārya, took out the right eye and gave it to her. Thereupon he brought the flesh and the brandy to his ācārya. On query he narrated the matter to the ācārya. The ācārya then demanded the left eye which was given. Thereupon the ācārya blessed him and in three years he got back his eyes like before. And in the same period he became a Mahāsiddha. He is called also Vairagīnātha. (pp. 123-124).

His disciple was Nāgo. Many Yogis regarded Karnari as identical with the king Bhanari. But they made a great mistake. As regards the Siddha Nāgo, he was called the naked because he did not have a thread as cloth on his body. When he stayed in the south, he came in the social-circle of the first wife of the king and gave her the Upadeśas. The king was angry, cut off the five limbs of the ācārya and thew them off towards the sky. But these limbs came back again and were fitted in the body. As this happened seven times, the ācārya in the end gave out a curse and the king's five limbs fell off by themselves, and then he died. But after a prayer for it he came back to life. Thus he showed his power. Then he disappeared towards the mountain Bhindapāla and there he is still living without throwing off his mortal body. (p. 124).

His disciple was the representative of the school of younger Virūpa Golennātha. As in the beginning he was confused on account of many Vinaya-laws, he withdrew himself and put himself in a big earthen pot. As it was not enough for him to acquire the Siddhi, he practised meditation by putting himself in one position (*Āsana*) and acquired the Siddhi in twelve years. Then he preached all sorts of Upadeśas to all who could understand them and went where Guru Nāgo dwelt and disappeared. (pp. 124-125).

His disciple was Oṅkāranātha, a son of a Kṣatriya from the country of Madhyadeśa. In his childhood he lost his father, and was brought up in the house of an elder brother. There Golennātha gave him a method to exorcise a Yogini. Besides this, he did not learn in eighteen years anything of science. Therefore, his brother and his wife drove him out with the words : 'You stupid, for what are you at all useful?' Being embittered he went in a strange country, lived on begging and began to exorcise the Vajrayoginī. He passed sixteen years on it, and a blessed voice arose in him and thus he came in the western country in the temple of Hiṅgatākṣidevī Umā. As he sat for six months contemplating on the stone-image of the Devi, and spread out a bright light from his body, the goddess became frightened and said: 'Oh Yogī, the fire of thy magical body is burning.' But he replied 'What shall I do with the magical powers or with the finding of a treasure? Surely I will take it when the Siddhi of the Vidyā is given to me; but it is not in the power of the goddess to give me the Siddhi, therefore, I must receive it from Gorakṣa.' Then he sought out Gorakṣa in the south and got the Siddhi. He gave his Upadeśas to the Mahāpaṇdita Ratigupta. (pp. 125-126).

Ratigupta was born in south India. By caste he was a son of a merchant. As he grew up he was converted to the teaching of the Bauddhas. He learnt with the representatives of all the schools and also was well-acquainted with the heterodox sciences. As he wanted to learn the Dharma of the Vajrayāna of the Guhya-Tantras, he visited the eastern countries and the islands of the sea, also he went in many western places. He prayed to Mahācārya Ratnakīrti, to Mahācārya Jñānagupta in the country of Ra-K'ang and the Nepāli Paṇdita Daśabala Laviṅha for the Abhiṣeka.

Once in a locality in eastern India there was a great festivity. There appeared a person carrying the hair-ropes like a Tirthika-Yogi and speaking suitably, he was asked who he would be. The answer was : 'I am Asitaghana.' From him he learned the magic-Upadeśa for a month. Also he heard the numerous Upadeśas from the Siddha Oṅkāranātha. Then he dwelt permanently in the three temple-cloisters in the south Viten, the country of Tarlarāti. He was firmly based on *Utpattikrama* and knew the fifteen Tantra-schools. (pp. 126-127). Here closes from the history, which is compared to a 'Mine of Precious Stones' the eighth chapter which narrates the tradition of various secret learnings." (p. 127).

"As regards the great Mudrā-possessor Śāntīgupta, who was a master of the magic-powers of these discoveries, was born in the city of Jalamaṇḍala which is in the south. As belonging to the Kṣatriya caste, from his youth he learned all the arts of his caste. He studied the dialectic with its complementary subjects (Aṅgas) and the language and was familiar with magic, as already his father had seen in dream the face of Bhaṭṭārikā-Tārā. He received also the Abhiṣeka of Tārā and learned the methods of exorcism. When he was twenty-two years old, there was in the country of Koṅkuna (Kaṅkana ?) on the bank of the sea, a cloister-institution called Suvarnadhvaja, which in former times was a good place

discourses one was giving six Upadeśas to the other as if these were answers to the questions. As they all disappeared in a wonderful way, Vajrayoginī and her companions made him a partner of it, and his Jñāna rose higher and higher. The place of his *Tattva* he did not know as yet ; but the disposition of his soul was towards such an ācārya, so that *Tattva* could appear to him. Therefore, he came to the door of a brandy-selling woman. But she took the form of a Vajrayoginī and said: 'In the southern country there lives an ācārya Jñānamitra by name; he will grant you the desired Śiddhi.' So the ācārya went to the south on foot and asked everybody but nobody could answer him.—(Translator).

"Once he met a man with the appearance of a householder Ārya who said that he himself was on the way to him ; that he lived in the city of Tipura which lay east from there. He asked him to lead him there. He said : 'If you have got the strength to tow all my belongings that are in the wood I will take you there.' He took the heavy load and the householder Ārya showed him the way. On the way Śāntigupta was captured by the robbers. As they wanted to divide the load, it became stone. Thereby the robbers became angry and repeatedly struck him so that he might fall on the ground like a dead man. Then appeared the ācārya again. He washed him with water and entered into conversations with him. Then he was refreshed and started again. As he came to Tipura, he prayed him to show the Guru, and when he was taken to the Guru on the bank of a small lake, his own picture appeared and said · 'That is Jñānamitra.' As he stood before him he got into a splendid Samādhi. When he prayed that Jñānamitra might take him as his disciple, this one answered : 'Thou art a shameless fellow that without money and honour, thou askest me to take thee as a disciple !' And becoming angry, he struck him many times. As the former one said : 'If I work with a rich man for thee then how much will I have for thee.' Then he said. 'Give one gold dinar everyday !' Thus he worked for a year long. People say that the field-worker in India is placed in especially wretched condition. Then followed various miraculous sufferings of the disciple Śāntigupta and deliverance. Both of them sailed for Ra-khine (Ārākān ?)." and later came back by ship.—(Translator).

"As the Guru from the beginning gave him no Upadeśas, he now prayed to give them to him and said . 'Gold and honour have I not, but let me follow you !' But the other said : 'Before a man, who poses as a rival and considers himself to be more than or at least equal to his Guru, Mahāśrīvajrasattva himself was terrified Thus one must humble himself !' Saying this, he showed much anger and went away."

Despairingly Śāntigupta sought death and threw himself from a stone but got no injury. Then he went to the place where the Śakti was bodily present.—(Translator).

"She said : 'The Guru came to my house, stopped here for a few days and has just gone to Nepal. ' With these words the woman completely disappeared. Then he brought himself to Nepāl. At last the sacrificing priest of the temple of Mahākāla in Jambu said that he had been here ; he had turned stupid things to stone and then had gone towards Kāmarupa. At once he started in his journey towards Kāmarupa. Finally, in the city of Garuḍaghāta in Kāmarupa he came to the place, where the ācārya had been with great joy. He made some hundred thousand prostrations by throwing himself on the floor. Then said the Guru : 'As you are desirous for the Upadeśas, here is the place from where my Guru Asitaghana went up to heaven ; there is the peak of the rock named Heramba, you make a *Stūpa* of bricks there as high as five men's height".

Then followed further miraculous trials till he found himself as a prisoner in the country of king Mukundadeva by his order. There were further trials till he found himself in a prison.—(Translator).

"Then Jñānamitra went to the door of the prison, threw dust on the warders and thereby all became lame. The door was opened by itself, Śāntigupta and more than five thousand prisoners became free. Then he followed the ācārya and came in a country called Triliṅga (Trikaliṅga?). Sarcely had he come in the city when the Guru gave him lots of the Upadeśsas. After two years said the Guru : 'Now is the time to give you the Abhiṣeka. In the house lying on the other side of the river, there lives a lady who is fit and prepared for all methods of the Tantras ; bring her to me.' Swimming in the evening he came to that house. It was the elephant-house of a Kṣatriya king, in the city of Laṅgakara. The girl belonged to the master of the house, as she was well-protected she could not be overpowered. The ācārya bound her by the magic-Dhāraṇīs, so that the woman might not speak a word. He put her on his shoulders and came away, and brought her before the Guru. The Guru said: 'Now it is the time' and on the morning he gave him the Abhiseka. For seven days long he gave him blessings and the uncommon oral Upadeśas. At that time their dwelling place was on a small hill. Formerly, the ācārya Nāgārjuna lived there. The people of the elephant-house who followed him, believed that both of them had been carried away by the water and did not come further. There he became the Mahesvara of the Yogīs. And this woman became a Yoginī. She followed the school of the Mīmāṅsakas and became famous as Yoginī Menakā. Her knowledge was as high as heaven, and later she acquired the Siddhi.

Then said the Guru Jñānamitra: "Oh Sāntigupta, I have made you know all the Upadeśas, you have the great ideal before you. Now you go to Soraṣṭa and work in the beginning without activity; then in hiding, then in coming out, try to make it with activity so that an event may take place.—All this time you work actively. Exactly at this time you, will acquire the rank of Mahāvajradhara."

After a further talk the Guru became invisible. (Translator).

"He served the Guru for ten years long. Then he (Sāntigupta) slowly went to Soraṣṭa in western India, bringing out deep thought in his longing songs, finally, sat in a place in deep meditation by giving up speech. It happened that the Tajiks and the Mongols during their march were throwing the stone and wooden idols in the fire, after they had burnt their cut-off hands and feet. He preserved as if without any feeling, and when a Hindu cavalryman, who was a believer, threw a mass of gold and silver-flowers, he remained as before as if without any feeling. Out of the mouth of my teacher came to me the information : 'It is not worthwhile to be seated stationary without any movement, but it is worthwhile to contemplate the Sūṇyatā, (शून्यता) when the question was for two years, that have passed, so it will be two and half years; the practices that are still necessary, I must make them up in six months'. Thus he practised that vigorously without activity. After he had been absolved he went through the cities and wards and there he secretly worked a little, for six months he carried the work of an Avadhūti, for six months a work for the children of the woods like that of a fool. In the meanwhile he preached Dharma also to the people of

of the ācārya. There was also a young
amed Gambhīramati. He went to the
and bound himself by duties to him.
eing a staunch believer and a disciple
ned there. As the ācārya saw that he
ainted with the *Pitakas*, he gave him
ṣeka and the Upadeśa. The disciple
l and within a short time won the
'seven miles-boot.'
the ācārya went to the country at
by his magical look made the Tirthi-
uskas, Mohammedans and Tajiks
nd like fate fell to the army of the
e country which he thus overthrew.
l the land for a long time so that the
of the people would be increased by
ing of the Dharma, and as in that
number of the Bauddhas was very
ought into existence the flourishing
He had six disciples who received
non Upadeśas: Paṇdita Vimalā-
drakara, Ratnakara, these three
ikṣu Panditas and further three
ka-Paṇdita Sugata, the Yoginī
l the Yoginī Tarikā. Thereby the
d in their possession the *Sampan-*
hey had the power to give out
create truth-attestations; these
sonally seen the face of Vajrayo-

of the city who regarded him as a man rich in knowledge, brought him gifts of various sorts. But in this country there was a king by race a Tajik; in the beginning he had only worst expropriations from the Bauddhas. But as there were a few Bhikṣus in this country, he believed later in the pious conduct of the Bhikṣus. But as the ācārya exercised the Tāntric practices, he did not like it. For that reason, he went to the ācārya and said: 'You fellow! do you speak lies or better speak the truth! would you bring disgrace to the Bauddha converts ?' Then the ācārya answered. 'On the face of the profits of these that we have perceived, we cannot change our character.' 'That you will just prove', said the king and let the ācārya be brought in the palace. There he sat completely alone on a high place, without food and no rooms to hide the utensils. The men, who watched him there, sat in a circle day and night near him. After seven days had passed without food and drink being given to him, and the condition of his body remained as before. The king let the beautiful girls come there from all over his country, thousands and perhaps more. Others say: Five hundred, came together and handed them over to the ācārya: 'As you know the practices of the

Tantras, so try to practise with them for a day.' Now the ācārya comprehended that according to the prophesy of the Guru the opportunity to work the practices of the Tantras with activity had come. He practised all the arts of the Śaktis with them and to show his power, he changed them all into dry skeletons. Being endowed with a glance like the sun, as the second sun directly arose from the height of the palace casting forth its rays far and wide, he went magically on the sky and put himself down in a distant park.

As the country became the best field of work, and there were Heteara in the country, he practised for six months long with activity, especially in Gaṇa-meetings. During the time of his stay in the hill called Ghirnari (Girnār?), the honours of the Siddhi of the highest Mahāmudrā came over to him. As these came in the time of early morning, there was a great earthquake, sweet smell filled everywhere, showers of flowers fell down, people heard music and singing from the sky. All men perceived that he saw the face of the Buddha of the tenth worldly region. At the same time, different protecting-gods and all the magicians appeared and sang blessing-songs. Seven days long the superhuman beings of the three worlds brought the Vīras and Dākas with in-

ginī. The Upâsaka Sugata acquired without hindrance the magic-powers and the four Karmas.

As the ācārya and these four went out together to visit the countries of thc east where the people of a Mohammedan Pāthān had brought a whole circle of countries in dire misery. The temple-cloisters of the Brāhmanas and the Bauddhas had all been destroyed, especially many Bauddha-cloisters on the mountain Devagiri on the sea-coast were turned into ashes. The temple of Khasarpana was set on fire, but it did not burn. As the ācārya and his spiritual brothers came there, he put them in prison with the words: 'In my country such shaven-heads with red coats had not been before, so it is also completely superfluous that you get yourselves settled here.' He let the hangman come as he wanted to kill them. But the other threw white mustard on the hangman and the prison-warders, who as thereby then became mad and senseless, they flew and came from there. By making a vow on Mahābodhi, they received the answer that the time was proper to act, in order to accomplish the tasks of terror. This was met by the ācārya and his four companions at Jārikhanda. They revolved the wheel of Yāmāntaka; then within six months the Pāthāns and the Moguls were innerly shaken and in the east all the followers of the religion of the Turuskas were slain in battle. The Hindu king Mānasing was taken prisoner.

Umāpati attained a rainbow-body. The Yoginī Tarikā worked with the four exorcism-glances without opposition. Then he cheated the Yogīs and the Yoginīs who followed the ācārya as disciples, all being twenty. After that he stayed in the south in Karnāta. The king of this country was a Tirthika. In order to convert him, he took him to his palace. In the interior of the palace there was a Liṇga terrible to look at, and it was established from the time of Arjuna. He treaded and danced on it and so his foot-prints were stamped on it. At this the king out of anger let six elephants be excited. In spite of the number of the elephants being six, who seized him with their trunks, he was not to be moved. As he threateningly raised his finger the stone image of the Chandikā, which once was of great miraculous power, melt away just like a lump of butter in the heat of the sun. Still now this figure remains there without becoming a mass. Then the king recognized, that he had acquired the Siddhi, and threw himself on the ground. After the news were spread on all sides that the ācārya possessed the Siddhi, the members of the Saṅgha of Mārahātā and Koṅkuna invited him and there he visited all their temple-cloisters. There he dealt out the Abhiṣekas and the Upadeśas and made the teachings of Vajrayāna very bright whilst he analysed the Tantras etc. Thirty Paṇditas and besides others, sixty in total, joined together as the four Parivāras, had only eleven men from the city not more as the perfect ones; the others were mostly in higher contemplation, and it happened that as soon as they attained the highest Siddhi, they became invisible.

Then the king of Bhandva invited him and gave him alms for a long time. He made also all the Bhikṣus assembled there from Suvarna-dvīpa, Paigudvīpa, Ra-Khan, Pu-Khaṅ and other distant islands, and again from Jambu-dvīpa all the Paṇditas as many as there were. He gave them all alms for three years. About three thousand Buddhist converts consisted the Upāsakas and the Upāsikās, again some hundred thousand of Yogīs from the four cor ners of the world prayed for the exorcism-method; others about the Upadeśas, some others performed the prayers for the Abhi-ṣekas and blessings, others again awaited with folded hands before the feet of the ācārya for the effect that would arise out of the changes. There were from the south the great Kaliṅga-

Paṇḍitas Vaidatikṣṇa Saṅghaśīla, from the country of Matyara the great ācārya Virabandhu and Asaṅgabodhi, from the country of Pañcadharavali, the ācāryas Anantamati and Vedānanda from the country of Re-khaṅ the great savants Dharmakṣaghoṣa and Parahitaghoṣa and the men from Vajrāsana Sumegha and others ; these prayed to the Māhācārya himself, with the Yoginī Dinakarā and with the spiritual sons of the Māhācārya viz. Māhācārya Gambhīramati for the profundity of the Tantra-books. Thus through the grace of the ācārya all those who confessed to Buddha from the Saṅghas of Āryadeśa took part in the grace of the Vajrayāna. But as in Vaṇadvīpa, Suvarṇadvīpa, Tamradvīpa etc. the Saṇghas contained only the Srāvaks and Saindhavas, they did not comprehend the word of the ācārya though he gave it.

During the time when the Guru from the eastern region of Nirvāṇaśrī found himself with the ācārya, the Māhācārya was stopping in a big bazar in Triliṅga. While some hundred thousands showed him respect. .There were many Bhikṣus from the islands, who came back from a visit from Māhābodhi. They spoke badly about all the secret Tantras, and they refused to honour the Māhācārya. Now, there was a king in Triliṅga, who held it necessary that many men, five thousand buffaloes, several thousands of birds, goats, sheep should be slaughtered as a sacrifice for Nātha Vikata. In order to make the preparation, he gathered hundred thousands of the Tirthikas and the Brāhmaṇs. As all these living beings were bound, there came the ācārya. It is incomprehensible by which way his magic-look was cast over all Brāhmaṇas and Tirthikas and they became benumbed and stiff. Being astonished the king came there. Then the ācārya spoke · 'If you kill all these living beings you will die at once, but after the death you will be born again in hell. So set them free.' Now as soon as they were set free the ācārya at once put his hand on his head and he was free from attacking; thereupon the people of the king became not less then the Yogīs and were completely endowed with the Vidyā.

Further was the Turuska king from the country of Canka. He went on the street near the place where the ācārya sat. As he used many abusive language to the ācārya and this was heard by one of his disciples, he gave out the curse. 'You all be dumb.' And the king and his people became dumb on the very spot. Then they were frightfully afraid and prayingly applied themselves to the ācārya. Then he said: 'To testify the power of the Bauddhas, all without exception you can speak again.' And thus it happened.

Further, in Bārānasi in Madhyadeśa there was a Tirthika-Paṇdita Madhusūdana Vasti who wanted to pass as a possessor of the Jñāna. In the midst of a large congregation he sat on a high throne; there the ācārya raised the fore-finger towards him and he fell down from the throne.

In the district of Mathurā there was a man who was called Mukundavartī. Formerly this one was a little bit of a Bauddha-Yogī. Later he became a Tirthika-Yogī. He exorcised the Ahuthacaṇdāli and it was glorified by it. He brought it to finish as he had brought many people within his power. By the glances of exorcism he destroyed them. As once the ācārya as a teacher with the disciples came to the city of Mathurā, he met together Mukundavartī and his followers who also went there. As thereby innumerable people from the city had assembled, the watchword was: 'But we will once see the magic-experiments of the both. This Mukunda who practised the magic-art of mass-hypnosis, had found believing followers in the kings of the Tajiks, Hamehunbāca (Humāyun Vādshah ?) and his son Akbar. But this time on account of the power of contemplation of the ācārya, he could not carry out any hypnosis. As soon as the ācārya had seen him with the glances of exorcism, he became mad, ran here and there shouting hā ! hā ! For seven days he could not become conscious and owing to the prayers of the ācārya he found himself normal again.

As the above-mentioned king of Bhandva died by this time, his son Balabhadra built before the door of the cavern, a big temple-cloister in which the ācārya had lived from time to time, and he presented it to him. He made a gift to him again with five hundred houses for the temple-slaves and during the time when five hundred Yogīs and Yoginīs were assembled, Ganacakras in big circumferences were made by them, while the king supplied the necessary things during three months. Few disciples were there at that time, and their spiritual bonds were loosened. From the first greeting with the Guru from the south (Nirvānaśrī) this fifth assembly was also the last.

Then he as a teacher became accessible to all, and thus passed seven years. While his oldest and best disciples had no connection with him, his body was changed into rainbow colours and his Jñānakāya clasped the heaven.

As regards him there are differences of opinions in general between the Tibetans and the Indians. Now what concerns Tibet, the opinion of those who critically work and give him the honourable title of a Siddha, would prove thereupon that he had acquired magical powers and the Karmacakrī. Then the magical-power and clear insight (Abhijñās) of all sorts as well as, all possible Dharmapālas as protecting gods he had seen. His spirit had needed a little light, and it was sufficient for his good consideration over the *Sǎmpannakrama*. And in India, though they confess that he had been a Siddha as far as he confined himself to the Siddha-signs, yet they deny that he possessed *Karmasiddhi*. Then his Siddhahood was confined to that much, that he had been a moderate Vidyādhara for the lower Siddhis, that he had been a pious Tāntrika, but it is confessed that he was no Siddha.

But this great ācārya brought in fourfold forms his tasks to end magically: Only through the word what he said took place, through the four glances of exorcism, in the midst of little refined congregations astonishment, and wonder-signs appeared on their faces and that he (in the Gāṇacakra) by the power of magic created thither flesh-balls, liquids, brandy and blood and the fruits of the woods. As he, therefore, appeared as the only guide of these things on the earth, they all praised him with the great name Śrī-sattvanātha with the words: 'Ārya has my teacher along with the Indians; three in all have heard the Dharma at the same time. Now it is sure that the Guru from the south (Nirvāṇaśrī) became the best Dharmaputra, so these especial teachers had received extended prohesies yet from the Mahācārya, the same from the ācārya Gambhīramati and from the Mahelvari of all the Yoginīs Dinakarā ; from these both had often got blessings and instructions. (pp. 127-148).

As regards the 'Driver of frights', it is doubtless that he was was one of the ten main disciples of the ācārya. As now in a Sūtra the development of history of this group of disciples is collected, therefore we shall mention him first.

In the country of Gujrātha Ghagha the intelligent son of a Kṣatriya was born. He prosecuted the studies of Language, Dialectic with the Aṅgas in the temple-cloister of Ābhu. He was converted and received the name of Gambhīramati. He knew completely the religious texts of the *Tripitakas*. Then as a ṅovice he came to the teacher at the age of nineteen years. When he became accomplished in the Tantras the Guru gave him the Abhiṣeka and the Upadeśas. Two years later he raised himself on the sure ground of the *Sampannakrama* stage and he received all possible knowledge for the highest stage. In order to earn riches and honour the ācārya acquired the Siddhi of 'seven miles-boots' for immediate exorcism. Entrusted with the methods learnt by the Guru, he received all the Abhiṣekas and the Upadeśas of his ācārya. At first he saw the face of Avalokiteśvara and that of Hayagrīva, then that of Mañjuśrī and Yamāntaka, thereafter of Hevajra and of Kurukullı. He made Mahākāli completely his servant, and he received everything that he ordered from the six great Yoginīs. (p. 149).

As regards the Yoginī Dinakarā, in the city of Cambhadatta in the south, there was a young prince named Harirasmi of the family of Pisila. He had a sister who from her youth was very intelligent and rejoiced herself in servıng virtues. After nine years, there appeared at the door a handsome bright Bhikṣu to collect alms. As she felt pain, he (the Bhisku) like those who were in want, begged for alms, and then said: I am not unhappy, while you are suffering yourself. It is said that anybody in the circle of Saṅsāra is bound to make mistakes, and there is also many possibilities of moral deficiencies of the Saṅsāra.' As she now prayed from him the means of the deliverance, she arrived directly at the main point of the Bodhisattva-conduct and on the method how to make ready the spirit of contemplation. As she comprehended it well and ten years had passed over it, she became the wife of a vassal prince of Kṣatriya blood of the country of Cavala and for thirteen years she knew the aim and the sense of the Saṅsāra. To her husband and the parents-in-law she always said words like the following : 'Why is it not then possible that I sit meditating on in my wide woods ; let it be permitted ! ' And in order to bring her from this, she was put at the head of household affairs. 'What for then to be a beggar where all things are staying in plenty at your command ? ' thus said the people of the house and the relatives. But she became an admirer of the people who went about a-begging. After it she showed herself as one crazed in mind, performed various asceticism, and put herself in a lonely place with a lady's maid. She overdid her former stupidities and separated herself from her husband. Man appointed time which was the fruit of the previous birth, lotus flowers and wheels (Cakras) came out in her hands and feet and thus as she was furnished with Lakṣaṇas, a prophesy came about her that when she could dwell, she would acquire Māhātmya. She heard that in a city of Mārahāṭā near Cavala dwelt the Mahācārya Śāntigupta. As soon as she heard his name, she felt a need for Samādhi and as soon as she saw his face, plunged into the complete Samādhi. During this time she had completed her twentieth year. Though a woman, she was of sharp intelligence, she knew the *Candravyākarana* complete, the *Abhidhānas*, the medicine and Dialetic of all forms. Through the inclination coming from such age she retained the seven hundred strophes and three hundred strophes of the *Prajñāpāramitā* through the simple recitation of the verse of the compendium. She understood well when she was asked about the aims to which a Bhikṣuṇi and to which a Upāsikā arrived at. The ācārya gave her the Abhiṣekas and the Upadeśas. For seven years she heard in the presence of the Mahācārya the discourses on Vajrayāna. By the Yoga, her power over the air became unparalleled She could ascend up the sky for miles. She also acquired the four magical looks. Then from the mouth of the Guru came the prophesy:

'From twenty years hence you will be equal to me.'

Once she went from Khagendra to the place called Raṅganātha by magic-powers. There were two temples: one belonged to the Brāhmaṇas and the other to the Bauddhas. There was a Maheśvara-Jaṅghama famous for his exorcism of the Bhairava. He knew the magic-power of the exorcising glances and destroyed the Buddha-Yogis. His name was Bhiṅgadeva. As he directed his exorcising glance on the Yoginī, it did not injure her, but on the other hand when she looked at him, he fell down and became breathless. When his health was restored again by a magic-glance, he became a believer in the religion of the Bauddhas.

Further, she met a Yogi named Ghamalavarma in Odivisa, who formerly could perform something, but later his vow was broken. He belied that he was a Siddha. By her magic-glance he got dysentery and vomited blood. Thus she destroyed the vow-breaker.

As soon as she wished she could see the faces of Śri-Heruka, the ten anger-gods and thirty-seven Vajrayoginīs, yet she did not attain the Siddhis of the highest kind.

This is thus the detailed news of ācārya Śantigupta and of his two main disciples. The third one was his Guru. From him he had acquired the grace to hear the Upadeśas on the Vajrayāna.

In India at first there had been hundred thousand sources which contained the knowledge of the Guhya-Tantras, but when Śri-Saroha appeared, they became comprehensible. During the time till the death of king Dharmapāla, there came a period when continually many Siddhas appeared, and the succession of the Siddhi followed without any interruption. Also, the succession of the Siddhas did not stop till the death of Abhayāṅkara. Afterwards there came a change as there was no more activity amongst those who came later on. Further, during the long period, in which appeared alone and without companions the later Siddhas and they were only Jñānamitra and Oṅkāranātha ; they brougt great help to the teaching of Buddha. Eighty years after the passing of Oṅkāranātha, Śāntigupta still acquired the Siddhis. When one ceased looking at the great or small advancement of especial kind, after the appearance of innumerble or smaller number of the Bauddhas, this ācārya Śntigupta especial in small or big advancement was equal only with Nāro, and therefore had the highest rank.

Here closes from the history which is equal to

a 'Mine of Precious Stones', the ninth chapter containing miscellaneous information as to how the Inspirations have come down." (pp. 127-153).

"In this book of seven Inspirations only a guiding-line for the blessing through the Siddhi dealt with is given, and only sixth chapter contains the main topic. One can experience in this writing the incomparable genealogy of the Gurus in the spheres of their subtle teachings. When I received the proposal to write on the endless redemption, only a part has been completed herewith, as I have not said about the redemption of many Tantra-Gurus. Here is written only on the basis of that which could be perceived from the histories prepared in India, and from that which were given in Tibet by the believing people, that were present from old times.

Now, elsewhere will be narrated other sorts of history of redemption in connection with the Mahāyāna-believers in India.

"If I have acquired reward by praising the *Jātakas* of the Gurus, many thereby of the living beings and the incorporeal beings also became the Bauddhas. I and all families and all, who always are at the service of all Gurus of this succession, may comprehend the secret of the soul." "There is present the wonderful path of the Vajradhara in seventh Inspiration, and a large number of his serving mankind in all worlds, and as this Yāna of the Ātman (spirit) is costly the teaching also may be capable of being redeemed, and the three worlds be freed from wants.

Blo-Idan Kun-dga rnam-rgyal, is the reviser, who had edited in *rNam-rgyal rab-tan* neighbouring the temple-cloister *dPal-sTag-hin-t'an* the excellent work completed by Tārānātha in his twenty-second year when he was the youngest servant of the order of his holy Lāmā, the work entitled the 'History Equal to a Jewel-mine'. That contains astonishingly wonderful *Jātakas* of seven Inspirations following one after another." (p. 153-154).

APPENDIX I

Notes by A. Gruenwedel

Mountain : Compare : Pañcasīrṣaparvata, Śrīparvata, Ghaṇṭāśaila, Devagiri, Khagendra, Dhinkoṭa, Ghirnari, Umāgiri, Phullahari, Kolamba, Heramba, I, loi.

Demons : Com : Amanuṣya Rakṣasa, Dākinī, Śūra, Bhuta, Ahuṭhacandālī Vīkata.

Fish : Com : Mina, Macchindra, Tilli, Kiṅgara, Śiśumāra.

Flesh : Com : Beef offered through Dakinī, pork flesh; human flesh. Compare : Mahāmāṅsa, flesh delivered in monasteries, flesh cut off from living body. Com : Dhama, Dhuma.

Gods : Brāhmaṇical : Umā, Hiṅgalāksṃī Umā, Caṇdikā, Viṣṇu Mahāviṣṇu, Jagannātha, Somanātha, Śiva, Iśvara, Liṅga, Kālidevī, Deveśvara, Maheśvara, Vairava, Yama, Vāsundhara, Viśvanātha.

Tantra-gods : Hevajra, Cakrasamvara, Candıkā, Vajravārāhi, Vajrayoginī, Bhattārikā-Ārya-Tārā, Mañjuvajra, Karmavajra, Hūṅkārā, Mārici Mahāmāyūri, Jambhala, Śrivajravairava, Hayagrīva, Vajradhara, Vajrasattva, Heruka, Śrī-Heruka, Kurukulli, Mahākāla.

Heterodox Brahmans : Drunk brandy, Lui-pā derided the Brāhmaṇas ; Brāhmaṇas who became Bauddhas : Saroha, Maitri, Kālavirūpa, Mahāpadmavajra, Kṛṣṇacāri, Śrīdhara, Tilli, Nāro, Jñānavajra, Vaidyapāda ; Brāhmaṇa-Tirthikas overcome by Dombi-Heruka. Nāro was a Tirthika before.

Witches : Com : Dākinī, Vajrayoginī, Vajravārāhi.

Further-India : Ra-Khāṅ, Pu-Khāṅ, Paigu-Dvīpa, Dhanaṣrī-Dvīpa.

Caste : No difference between higher and lower castes : twelve castes. Com : Dombi, Candāla-girls.

Cloisters : Vikramśila, Nalanda, Eḍapura, Ābhu, Suvarṇa-dhvaja, Somapuri, Takṣaśila, Vajrāsana, Otantapuri, Dharmāṅkurāraṇya, Jagddala, and Devikota.

Monk : Com : Bhikṣu, Śrāvāka, Saindhava, Saṅgha, Hiṅayāna, Pitaka, Tripitaka, Vinaya, Brāhmaṇabhikṣu, Śrāmanera.

Statue : Com : Stone figure, Statue of sandal of Tārā, Statue of Heruka, of copper, Silver statue of Heruka, of Somanātha,

Avalokiteśvara over it, of Avalokiteśvara, of Viṣṇus, of Mañjuśrī, of Umā, Statues of gods fetched, Statue of Caṇḍikā.

Dance: Dombi-dances, dancing-girls of the gods; dancer and singer, mystic dance of the Tāntrikas.

Temple: Nāgas built temple, dedication of temple, Temple-priests. Heterodox temples: Jagannātha, Somanātha.

Mirror: Rock-mirror, Hell shown in mirror, mirror in Harem, of Antarabhāva.

Transformation: Into a jackal, into a horse. Com: Aśvapāda; into stone, into cats, statues transformed themselves into dust. Com: Gopicandra, water into a drink, Gazelle into a tiger, dog into a woman, Brāhmaṇas and Brāhmaṇīs into witches, Vajrayoginī into Caṇḍāla-girl, Yoginīs into bathing-hetaera, woman into a cloak, son and daughter into thunderbolt and cloak, heads of the Dakinis into sheep-heads, sesame into melting-butter.

Woman: As: Mudrā, Śakti, Vidyā, Yoginī, Śakti as good, and as the Guru. Women for the function of a Yogi, woman stolen for Guru, Candāli-woman to the Gaṇacakra, sandal-rubbing women as Padmini, Śakti of Mañjuśrī. Com : Padmini, Hetaera, Dinakarā, Tarikā, Menakā, Guneru, Jatijālā, Bhajaduru, Candraprabhā, Lakṣmikarā, Vilasyavajrā, Cintā, Mekhalā, Kanakhalā, Sahajasiddhi-girls, Subhogā, Gaṅgādhari, Padmāvati or Logi, Jñānavati or Guṇi.

Magic : Magic-circle (Maṇdala) of Āryatārā, of Vajravārāhi, of Cakrasamvara, of Heruka, of Samvara and Hevajra, of Mañjuvajra, of Mañjuvajrasamāja, all Tantras, Naro's blood-maṇdala ; magic-glances, four glances, magic-body. Com : Vajra burnt a goddess ; magic-words, magic-formulae : Dhāraṇis, a woman bound through Dhāraṇi, set aside jugglery of the heterodox persons; heterodox and Bauddha-magic, Dhāraṇis of the Dakinīs; of Guhya-Tantras, of Mahākāla, of Kurukulli, of Mahāmāyurī, of Pha and Mātṛ-Tantras, Matṛkadhāraṇis magic-hyp-nosis by the heterodox Dhāram, heterodox Dhāraṇi brings rain, magic-benediction of Nāgārjuna and Udayāna. Magic-texts; Tantra-magic which do not contradict the Piṭakas, Tantra-handbooks, Tantra-commentaries, Tantras of the south, Vijegiri-Tantra, Dākini-Tantra, Vidyā -Tantra, Tantras of the Mahākāla, of Guhyasamāja, Guhya-Tantras, Tantras of Nāgārjuna, of Lui-pā, of Maitri, of Dombi, of Lakṣmikarā etc, of Indrabhuti and Padma, bad Dākini- Tantras, Tirthika-Tantras ; Magic-powers, Magic-influence on wood, Magic-sleep, small Siddhis, great Siddhis ; magician, an accomplished Tantrika-Siddha.

Mahasiddha : The names of the following Mahāsiddhas are given in Grub t'ob (Tānjur Fol. of the Tantras, which are numbered there, are put down below ; the names and legends sometimes differ) : Lui-pā (1), Virupa (3), Dombi-pā Tārānātha. Dombi-Heruka, (4), Śavari-pā (5), Saraha-pā (6), Mina-pā (8), Gorakṣa (9). Tsanrāṇga-pā (10), Vina-pā (11), Canti-pā (12), Tanti-pā (13), KLusgrub; Nāgārjuna (16), Nag-po-spyod-pā, Kṛṣṇacāri (17), Karnari-pā (18), Thagana(19), Nāropā (20), Tillo-pā : Tilli (22), Bhadrapā (24), Kambhala : Kambala (30), Diṅkapā : Diṅki (31), Bhande-pā (32), Kukkuri-pā (34), Dharma-pā (36), Indrabhuti (42), Kotali (44), Jalandhara-pā : Jālandhari (46), Ghaṇṭa-pā : Vajraghaṇta (52), Tsaluki-pā : Cilu ? (54), Carpati-pā : Tsa-pa-ri-pā (64) Mekhalā (66), Kanakhalā (67), Dharikā-pā : Dārikā (77), Lakṣmikarā (82), Vyāli-pā (84), Nirguna : Naguna ? (57), Saroruha : Sāgara, Sakara (74).

Lui-pa : Lui-pā is the Tibetan abbreviation of Indian Lui-pāda. In the Grub t'ob the legend of Lui-pā is narrated in a different way ; the reason why he ate fish-entrails is given there. Originally he was a prince. He had still the caste-pride remaining in him, because when a Dākinī gave him bad food, he threw it away. He recognized this hesitation and scruple to be hindrances to his Bodhi, therefore, he atoned with such bad food.

Virupa : The goddess Candikā rescued him from the Gaṇas by absorption, who wanted to kill and consume him first out of a mass of human-sacrifices. Compare such similar situation with Willian Taylor : Oriental Manuscripts in the Government Library ,Madras II,

(1860, p. 887). According to Grub-t'ob where he appears in No. 3, he first rescued a young Brāhmaṇa from the flesheating Dākinīs thereby, he gave him the blessing.

Bhanvadala : The name of the elephant of king Ramāpāla is also to be found in Sum-Pā-Khan I-Poh, p. 104.

Tilli : Regarding the appearance of Tillī as a dark-skinned man frying living fishes in the kitchen, it is all very well to remember the well-known story in "*Thousand and One Night.*"

Nagarjuna : Regarding the tree-leaves shoes of Nāgārjuna it is to be remembered that Vararuci also possessed such shoes. Vide Translation of Tārānātha by Sachiefner, P. 55.

Chaurangi : Com : Mollesworth Mārāthi English Dictionary P. O Chauraṇgi and the words derived from it. It means as 'a man who is bundled on a stool' as his hands and feet are cut off. Com. Sanskrit Pitha, Sarpin and Jātaka (Ed. Fausboell, VI, 4, 14, 5, 12); a parallel appearance is the 'Schameler' in 'Spielmanusepos' of the middle ages of Europe.

Jambala : A Yakṣa.

Jalandhari : Com: Sarat Ch. Das: 'A Note on the Antiquity of Chittagong, Journ. As. Soc. Bengal, LXVII, 1898, No 1, P. 20ff quoting Sum pa-khan-Po I, 109, line 9 ff where it is said: 'Jalandhari or Bālapāda was born in the Śudra caste, in the western country of Sindhu, in a city which was called Nagara Thatha.'

Saroruha : A Kṣtriya and a Paṇdita who became the Purohita of a king.

INDEX